DIAMONDS IN THE VALLEY

The Intriguing Story of a Family's Triumph over Adversity

Mike and Bev Case

Scripture References

Versions of the bible used by the authors in the book are:
New International Version (NIV)
King James Version (KJV)
Unless otherwise stated, scriptures quoted are from the NIV

Illustrations by Alfanso Fraser and Deborah Case

DIAMONDS IN THE VALLEY - Revised Edition
Copyright © 2013 by Mike and Bev Case

All Rights Reserved

No part of this book may be reproduced in any form and by any means without written permission of the authors

DEDICATION

To the honor and Glory of the Sovereign God of the Universe whose providence, inspiration and anointing gave us the vision and determination to start and complete this project

AND

To the memory of our most wonderful mothers; Linda Case and Petra King, whose faith, courage, determination and kindness helped to lay the foundation for us to triumph over many of life's valleys

Acknowledgements

It is with a deep sense of gratitude that we convey our sincere thanks to a number of persons who were instrumental in bringing this revised edition to fruition:

Thank you Karo for your editorial services, and your timely advice on context and formatting.

Thanks to our many brothers and sisters in Christ who stood with us in prayer, among them were: Flo, Pam, Karo, Autherine, Leaford, and Anthea.

Thank you Autherine, Dennis and Karen for accepting the challenge of handling all our business affairs in our absence.

Thank you Percy for your words of encouragement that God would continue and complete what He began in us.

Thank you Pastors Al and Melody for your constant counsel and concern for our general welfare.

Thank you sister Pam for your motherly admonition, encouragement and advice.

A big thank you to our children for support, prayers, and believing in what the Lord is doing in and through us.

...What others are saying...

Books about people who triumph over severe adversity are in demand. They must be, in these depressed times, and the more familiar the story, the more we are attracted to the book...Faith in any form is the basis of overcoming depths, and that is what makes the book appealing.
The Jamaica Daily Gleaner

Diamonds in the valley has something for even the most discriminating reader. In this slim, easy to read volume you will find comedy, action, suspense, drama, romance, illustrations and even family portraits and a story full of life's lessons. It is a story many will be able to identify with.
The Love Herald

Today, more than ever, many believers seem to be having "valley experiences." This is therefore a timely work out of the experiences of the Case family, set in our modern world...May this book be an inspiration, encouragement and challenge to you as you read it.
Rev. Dr Al Miller
President, Whole Life Ministries and
Pastor, Fellowship Tabernacles

Jamaica's sociology is enriched when local stories get told and even more so when the authors come from 'inside' organizations rarely penetrated. Michael and Beverly do have a story worth telling, and they have told it with honesty, analysis and testimonials that make it a book well worth reading, particularly by people interested to know the 'workings' of small churches with strong control tendencies.
Rev. Dr Billy Hall
Journalist, Evangelist and Social Analyst

PREFACE TO THE REVISED EDITION

Diamonds in the valley was written for readers who are currently experiencing, or have in the past experienced severe and prolonged; trial, testing and dislocation. It was especially written for those who have never been able to view their suffering from the perspective of eternity. It is the true story of the Case family, recounting their journeys, frustrations, hopes, dreams and triumphs. Their journey from country to country and from city to city, their quest for answers to life's perplexing questions.

During the final stages of publishing the first edition, it became apparent that there were gaps in the chronology of *Diamonds in the Valley*. The period between the Case's return from Trinidad and Beverly's illness gave birth to the chapter *Repatriation in the Valley*. It was on that basis among others that the idea of another edition was born.

Since the first launch in April 2001, much has happened to further the Case's intriguing story; a musical drama inspired by and named after the autobiography *Diamonds in the Valley* was staged by the drama group *Destiny* in the summer of 2001, a sponsored promotional Caribbean tour by the authors in May 2002, and television and radio interviews locally and abroad. This in conjunction with the sense that there was a need for a chapter detailing some of the victorious restoration to the Case family gave birth to another new chapter *Restoration in the Valley*. It then became obvious to those involved that the ministry of *Diamonds in the Valley* was not yet complete.

Care was exercised to ensure that the original purposes of the book remained intact; that of offering hope and encouragement during times of adversity, highlighting the diamonds to be mined in life's valleys, recounting the many valley experiences of the Case family and from a biblical framework looking at the many lessons learned, insights gained and victories won from them. This was written with an emphasis on seeing these valley experiences through the eyes of the biblical pattern.

CONTENTS

Chapters

Formed Diamonds

1	Childhood in the Valley	1
2	Romance in the Valley	15
3	Lessons in the Valley	23
4	Philip in the Valley	37

Rough Diamonds

5	Bandits in the Valley	45
6	A Sovereign God in the Valley	51
7	Pilgrimage in the Valley	59

Mined Diamonds

8	The Church in the Valley	77
9	Repatriation in the Valley	91

Finished Diamonds

10	Beverly in the Valley	101
11	Restoration in the Valley	119
12	The Light in the Valley	127

Epilogue   137

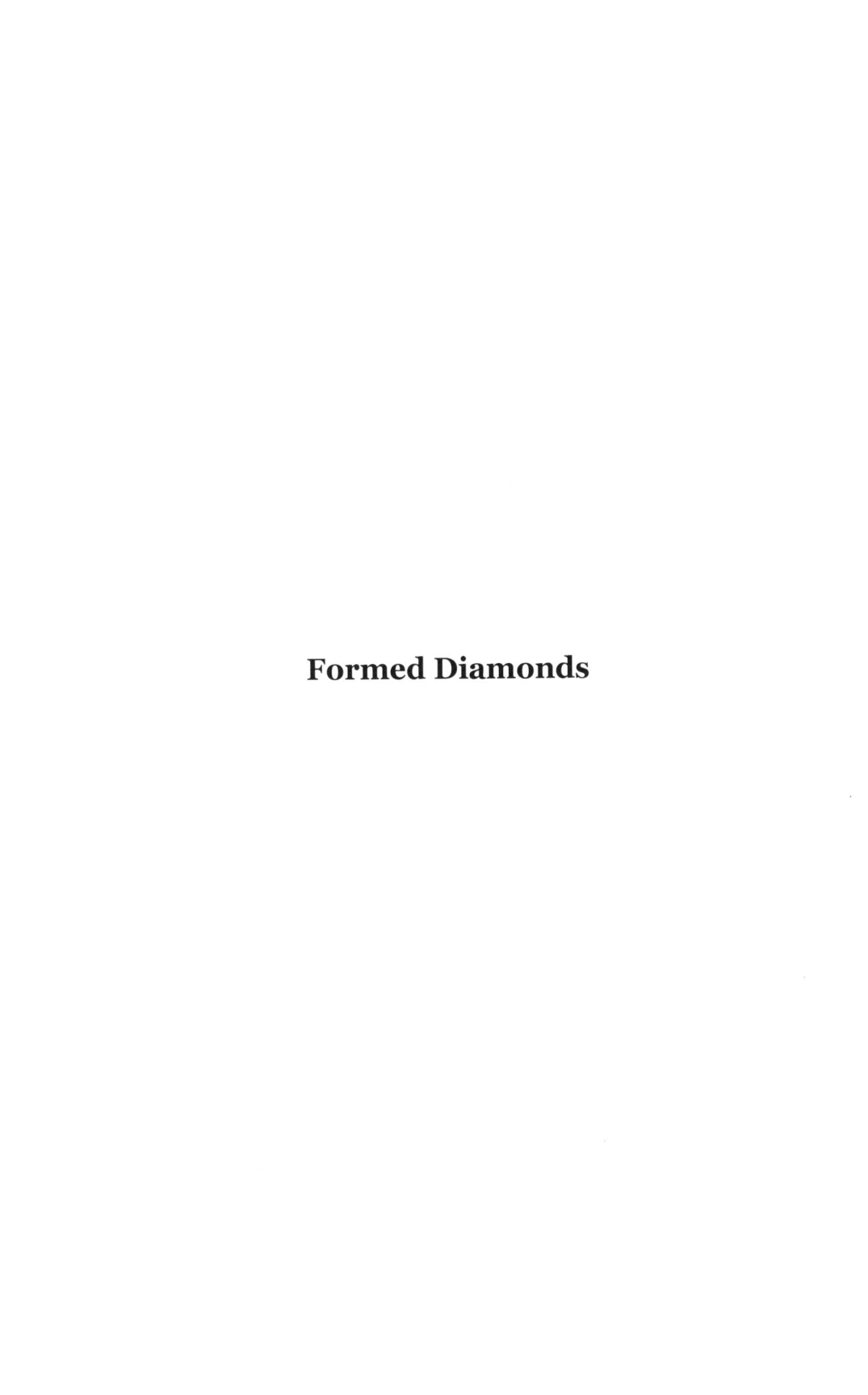

Formed Diamonds

Diamond is the hardest natural substance on earth, and is extremely resistant to tarnishing

1

CHILDHOOD IN THE VALLEY

Mike
During the early sixties there was hardly a dull moment in the life of the Case family of 31 Whitehall Avenue, Kingston 8, Jamaica.

I was the seventh child of eleven born to Lester and Linda Case on the seventh day of the seventh month, 1953. At birth I weighed seven pounds. From as early as I can remember I have always felt that this series of sevens entitled me to a special life of some sort, and this feeling was reinforced when I got married in '77 and when I fathered seven children. And what a special life it was going to be!

My parents were one of a kind. Papa, my father, was a strapping six-footer. He was the quiet meditative type who left the bulk of the talking to my mother Mama, who was just over five feet tall but quite a personality.

Papa seems to have tried a variety of jobs, going from army sergeant to businessman and then to civil servant. He was in and out of multiple episodes of what was loosely defined back then as "nerve problems" but later diagnosed as schizophrenia. Mama, a noted seamstress in the community, was the business brain of the family.

Papa had passed through high school and was a talented artist and chemist. He once founded a firm that produced flavours and essences that he sold around the country, travelling in a land rover. He was the nation's leading cartoonist after the Second World War, and at one time as a cartoonist had worked for a leading daily newspaper in Kingston. He later retired as a civil servant, an assistant director at Cobbla Youth Camp in Spaulding Manchester.

Mama did not make it to high school, but being largely self-taught could engage in any meaningful conversation with anyone on any issue pertaining to everyday life.

Trevor, the eldest child, was acutely aware of his status as heir apparent and would often bully his two younger brothers. He prevented them from complaining about his misdeeds with threats of reprisals.

Sweet revenge came their way one summer day when the three boys, all in their early teens, were bird shooting. Derrick sighted a dove on a nearby guango tree. He alerted Beres, and the two boys started stalking the bird. Trevor got wind of what was happening and decided as usual that he should take the shot. "Leave it to me" he affirmed as he pushed both boys aside. With the crook of the slingshot in his right hand and the left on the tongue that held the rubber, he positioned himself under the bird and was about to fire when the rubber band snapped, hitting him in the eye. For a moment he went blind and began to bawl.

Derrick and Beres then saw an opportunity for sweet revenge. Trevor was in a frightened frenzy. They took him aside and reminded him that with faith all things are possible. Leading him by the hand they took him to the edge of the gully bank. There, they reminded him of the bible story that Papa had related in family worship. The story was that of a blind man that had gone to Jesus for healing, and Jesus had spat on some mud and used it to heal the man of his blindness.

The two younger brothers proceeded to gather mud from the gully and used the mud to plaster their older brother's head and eyes. Trevor in his frightened condition was unaware that his two younger brothers were grinning from ear to ear as they were seemingly helping him. They led him by hand from Army Bush, Havendale, across Upper Ward Lane to Whitehall Avenue, singing the sweet refrain of a song they composed:

> "Jus' because the bingie never tie, it pop and lick 'im in 'im eye."

Derrick and Beres were a couple years apart and grew up like twins, but despite this they still played pranks on each other. Beres the younger was tall, muscular and well built. Derrick was small, skinny and very witty.

One day Beres was rewarded with a bulla cake for some good deed he had done for Mama. Derrick took him aside and counselled him to bury the bulla cake, assuring him that by the next morning a bulla tree would grow, and he would have not just one but many. Beres fell for the idea. They dug a hole, buried the cake and poured water all over it before retiring for the night.

In the wee hours of the morning while Beres slept, Derrick got up, dug up the bulla cake, brushed off the dirt and devoured it.

It was the bane of our lives that there were no mango trees in our yard, though all the neighbors around us had plenty to spare. As children we had convinced ourselves that we were like the children of Israel with lands around us being the Promised Land flowing with milk and honey, and ever so often we would lead expeditions across the fence to claim this booty. Innovative ideas were not in short supply as we lead expeditions by night and by day to pick these forbidden fruits.

Trevor seems to have been always enticing others to do the risky work while he stayed behind supervising from a comfort zone. On one occasion, however, he ventured up Mrs Smith's mango tree nearby our fence in search of ripe mangoes. Unknown to him was the fact that Mrs Smith had not yet left for work and appeared under the tree asking, "What are you doing up there, son?"

Derrick and Beres came on the scene and with laughter in their voices jeeringly questioned Trevor loudly, "Why is it that your kite is perched so close to the mellow mango?" Of course there was not even a trace of any kite near the scene.

Another strategy used was to throw a shoe across Mr Brewster's fence, and on retrieving it, gather a few fruits on the way back. On one particular attempt we were not so fortunate, as I was nominated to be the one to retrieve the shoe. As I descended the sash-window ledge, up came Mr Brewster with the shoe in his hand and handed it back to us. Our brief expedition to 'Canaan' was aborted.

In retrospect it was hard to imagine how as a family with parents being such devout Christians and upright and respected members of the community, teaching their children in the ways of the Lord, conducting family devotions at least weekly, and so on, we could have devised these mischievous plans without second thought. It was an enigma.

As a boy I had an insatiable appetite for boiled eggs, so I became an expert at discerning the different sounds of the neighborhood hens. I watched a particular brown hen one day, and as she got up from the nest underneath Mr Guppy's house and began cackling, indicating the laying of another egg, I was over his fence in a flash. There were several eggs in the nest. I took them all, loaded up my two side pockets and headed back over the fence.

On re-entering our yard, I became uncomfortably aware of a tall dark six-footer standing at the back door with a serious look on his face, and his right hand behind his back clutching a long dark dangling object. I was caught in the act. I had no alibi, and it made no sense running away. Where would I go? If I ran the punishment would have been doubled. So I did the only sensible thing, and after submitting myself to the 'Laying on of hands,' lost my appetite for eggs.

Most of this time was before the advent of television, videos or computers, so we children had to find innovative means of entertaining ourselves. Story-telling, a lost art to our modern day counterparts, was one such means. We also indulged in cricket, football, "neck-back bingie war" and putting on skits at Christmas time.

"We grew up a very close-knit family. Papa and Mama were our role models"

As a family we were always financially challenged. So, even to purchase a ball to play cricket could sometimes be out of our reach. On one such occasion we decided to use a green mango as a substitute cricket ball to play a game. Paul, my senior brother by two years, along with Chris and Karl, both younger, were playing. The game was very exciting and within the hour Paul skied the ball over the housetop onto the other side. Chris went to recover the ball, but found that by then the mango had softened considerably, giving the appearance of a ripe fruit. After a few minutes without seeing him appear from around the house, we went in search of him and the ball. We encountered him sitting on a log making a meal of the ball. With the absence of the ball, the game ended in a draw.

Another form of entertainment we devised was "playing court" Perry Mason style. Once during summer break someone made an incredible mess in the bathroom that left Mama furious. Paul and I visited the scene and decided that it was time for court. We summoned Dicky and Cliffy, our neighborhood playmates, and played. Paul was judge, Cliffy was defence attorney, Dicky was bailiff, Patty my younger sister was court reporter and Karl and Karlene, the twins, were the courtroom audience. We set out to solve the mystery of the messy bathroom. I was prosecuting attorney and Chris was chief suspect and so he took the stand.

The arguments were convincing as the prosecuting attorney tried to prove him guilty. The cross examinations were intense and furious. As the courtroom drama heated up, Cliffy apparently forgot his role as defence attorney and started shooting questions at the accused. All the evidence seemed to point to Chris and with no advocate he broke down and confessed to the 'crime.' We all led him to Mama for sentencing; but to our disappointment she granted him mercy.

Despite occasional skirmishes we grew up a very close-knit family. Papa and Mama were our role models. I had never witnessed them arguing in front of us children. They had set forth a sterling example of Christian living.

Family worship was conducted most evening around the family dining table. Papa read from the scriptures and expounded on its everyday application. He often referred to the neighbors' mangoes as the 'forbidden fruit.' We listened keenly to Papa, especially as marshmallows from Captain Townsend of the Salvation Army were used as incentives for those who paid careful attention.

Mama played a supportive role and was a woman of incredible faith. I was probably too young to remember, but once when Papa was ill and there was no food in the house, she asked Maxine, my older sister to put the pot on the stove.

Bewildered, Maxine pointed out that there was no food to cook, to which Mama replied "The same God who gave me these children will provide food for them." The pot of water had hardly started boiling when brother Metzler, a Mennonite missionary working in the community, appeared at the front door with a bunch of green bananas in his left hand and a box of groceries on his right shoulders. We were amazed at Mama's demonstration of faith and God's goodness.

Life today is a struggle, but I believe the legacy of perseverance, faith and faithfulness left by our parents has served us well in helping us face today, the dark valleys. I had never known Papa to stop and drink with friends on the street. He would hand his entire pay check over to Mama.

Despite the struggles, we were happy because we were together and because we valued each other. There was a family spirit of love, openness and camaraderie that money could not buy. I would not trade my childhood experiences for all the riches in the world.

Papa was never a demanding father. He ate whatever was provided with thanksgiving. He enjoyed the comforts of his children combing his hair and plucking the grey hairs from his head; and so a typical scene at home at leisure time would see Papa sound asleep on his back with Flo and Maxine combing and plaiting his hair, Paul cutting his finger and toenails, and I perched on his chest plucking the grey hairs from his chest and head. In spite of the fuss and confusion, Papa would still be in deep slumber.

Papa's older brother Charles O. Case, affectionately called Uncle Charley, was one of those rare souls who was always there for us in our times of need. Uncle Charley ran a successful mechanic establishment on Mark Lane in Kingston, and if there ever was a genuine saint, he was. It is said that he had the unique ability to listen not just with his ears but with his heart. Never much of a talker, but his silent understanding presence was always felt by those whose lives he had touched.

As I grew in my teen years, I became more aware of the need to begin thinking about my future. My parents were a great influence on me during those years and at a particular family worship session, I made an open commitment and profession of faith to serve Jesus Christ as Lord and Saviour. I believe to a large extent the example of my father was a deciding factor, for I wanted him to be proud of me. This sincere experience of my early years has lasted. I do not believe at the time, that I was fully aware of all that discipleship meant, but I did put my trust in Jesus.

Swallowfield Primary school on Whitehall Avenue became the institution of early education to all the Case children. Mr Roberts, the Miller sisters, Mr Clark and Mr and Mrs Riley were some of our early educators. The primary goal of these schools was to prepare us to sit the Common Entrance or Technical School exams that would allow us free or near free passage to a Secondary education.

In 1965 I sat the Common Entrance exam, but was awarded what was called a half scholarship, meaning that I would have to find funding for half the school fees. That would have been a burden on my parents; as a result I sat the Technical School exam the following year and surprisingly was awarded a place at Kingston Technical High School, KTHS. I had applied for St Andrew Technical High School, STATHS, because I had a long legacy to protect.

You see, Derrick was one of the first students enrolled at STATHS in 1961, then before he graduated Maxine started attending, so despite KTHS being the more popular choice, I desperately wanted to attend STATHS. As fate would have it, six of us Case children; Derrick, then Maxine, then me, then Heather (Patty), then Charles (Chris) and then Karl attended. There was an unbroken period of over fifteen years when there was always a Case child in attendance at STATHS, a record to this day.

I spent the first week of the school year of 1966 at KTHS and immediately applied for a transfer which was granted. I remember only a few names from there, particularly a classmate whose last name was Zinc. We became friends because at last I met someone with a more peculiar last name than mine. Rookwood was another boy I remember.

I entered STATHS the following week in Form 1C. I never really excelled at my studies, just an average student who had a keen interest in playing cricket. Hoping someday to make my school's team, then my country's team, then hopefully to be a West Indies star like Garfield Sobers or Frank Worrell. Beres, who had represented Meadowbrook High School in the Sunlight Cup cricket competition, had spent time coaching me how to bat, bowl and field. In 1C my friend Gladstone was a guy from the country areas with a strong rural accent. I enjoyed listening to this guy talk. His accent was so pronounced, it sounded like a foreign language. My grades were just about average then. I believe my mind was more on cricket and sports than on getting a sound education.

Shortly after the second term began in January 1967, I was diagnosed with Acute Nephritis, a childhood kidney disease, and was admitted to the University College Hospital. I was not aware of how serious it was, but Flo, who by then had graduated nursing school from the same hospital, updated Mama on the seriousness of the disease. By the second week, I had fallen into a coma, which lasted for one week. Few thought I would have pulled through. My friend Gladstone told me months later that they had announced my passing at school, STATHS, one morning. Not sure if he was joking or serious, but it was that critical.

"I awoke from my coma a week later to be aware of a bed-board and a porter stationed at my bedside in Ward 4"

I awoke from my coma a week later to be aware of a bed-board and a porter stationed at my bedside in Ward 4. My attending nurse, Hazel Field Ridley, a short, dark, pleasant girl from Guyana, for whom I had a very serious crush, was ever so attentive to me. She would take some of her batch mates to visit me at nights after her day shift ended. We always seemed to smile in each other's presence. She referred to me as her little boy friend, a designation that filled my stomach with butterflies.

During the two months stay at UCH, there were three VIPs also admitted: Mr Hugh Crosdale, a weather forecaster at JBC TV, who had a rare blood disorder, a government politician, Mr Wakeland and lastly my hero Frank Worrell, the great cricket captain of the West Indies team.

Mr Wakeland died before I had an opportunity to visit his room. I made several visits to Mr Hugh Crosdale's room, and we became friends. I had high hopes of visiting Sir Frank Worrell, but early one morning I saw that dreaded metallic box being wheeled from the direction of Ward 8 along the corridor, and nurse informed me with tears in her voice that Frank Worrell had passed the night before. My hopes of visiting this great hero and sportsman were dashed. Nurse held me in a close embrace as she comforted me during one of the greatest disappointments of my life.

I was discharged from the UCH in mid-March 1967 with strict instructions to stay away from salt and all strenuous activities. I had to re-evaluate my plans for cricket as a result. I had to have complete bed rest for several months, so any plans of resuming school were also dashed. I thought that my life was over. What would I do? My hopes of representing my school, country and region had suffered a severe blow.

I was readmitted to STATHS in first form, 1B in 1967 at its resumption after the summer break that year. It was then that I developed a love for books, or more appropriately knowledge. I chose the engineering option, moving from 1B to HE21, then HE31, then HE41 before graduating in 1971.

Despite having four sisters, I grew up somewhat insecure when around girls. I dated on a very few occasions while at STATHS. During one summer, I double dated to Hope Gardens with another couple from my batch. I escorted another batch mate to our graduation ball, and shortly after STATHS I dated another batch mate who I had liked since third form, for several months. I had a flawed exit strategy, however, so as soon as I perceived; real or imagined, that this relationship could have negatively impacted my academic goals, I ceased abruptly. I never gave a reason or an apology for my action. As I matured in later life and considered the possible impact of my actions, I regretted the crude manner with which I handled these delicate situations.

I enlisted in the cadet corps at STATHS with the hope that this weekly activity would not be too much strain on my recovering kidneys. Derrick was a lance corporal during his time there as a cadet. John Austin Holmes had retired as principal at the end of the first year, and Mr Copeland, an interim principal from the UK, took over for a year, but STATHS really came into its own at the arrival of Mr S. W. Isaac-Henry at the beginning of my third year.

Zacky, as he was affectionately called, was an educator par excellence. He encouraged us all to be everything that we could be in life. It was then that the idea of becoming an engineer was born, blossomed and flourished. I had to make some serious decision during this period as we began preparations in earnest for the General Certificate of Education (GCE), Associated Examining Board (AEB), Ordinary Level (O'level) exams.

Zacky was an ardent supporter of the cadet corps at school, being a colonel himself of the corps, so one of the most difficult tasks I faced was to explain to him and 'Daddy' Wilkins, our commanding officer and Technical Drawing teacher, that I had to quit the corps to concentrate on my studies. I had risen in rank to become one of two sergeants in my third year, the other being Joida Francis, who later became Sergeant Major and Head Boy. So at the end of my third year at school I resigned from the cadet force.

Along with my study partner Fuller, who I knew from Swallowfield Primary, I planned on sitting nine subjects that year. Attaining nine subjects at the AEB O'level, was unprecedented at any Technical High School in Jamaica to date, so we had to be focussed.

I had developed a voracious appetite for knowledge, especially in the fields of Maths and Science. I excelled in my exams. Despite the fact that I believe anyone of several guys could have been awarded that one Technical Scholarship that year, among them; Fuller, Victor, Brooksy, Miguel, Keith and Wesley, just before graduation from high school, I was awarded the 1971 Jamaica Technical High School Scholarship that led me on a path to become an engineer.

I spent one year at UWI Mona, pursuing preliminary studies, and then left for Trinidad and Tobago the following year to finish my course.

Mama later confided in me that my being awarded the scholarship was one of the proudest moments of her life. It was a real bright spot in an otherwise struggling life. I remembered her repeating the Magnificat of the book of St. Luke chapter one.

There were several persons who contributed greatly to my development in the formative years. Three of them stand out.

My father, Papa is one. He taught us by his own lifestyle and involvement in our lives. He taught me the values and virtues of life. He was and still is my hero. He set the tone for me to be the kind of man that I became. He was always there for his family and would sacrifice his own comforts in ensuring that all our needs were met.

"Despite our lean financial circumstances, many were the neighborhood kids that she fed from her kitchen window"

My mother, Mama was always there nurturing and comforting. Whenever we children fell ill, she would literally not sleep that night in seeing to it that we had all the comforts that we needed. She was the embodiment of giving, and despite our lean financial circumstances, many were the neighborhood kids that she fed from her kitchen window. No one could sit down to Christmas dinner until several elderly people of the Whitehall community were first given a portion of the family's meal, including all the trimmings.

S. W. Isaac Henry was another major influence on my life. He was principal of St Andrew Technical High School for many years. Zacky was a dynamo of sheer energy. He believed in all his students and motivated us to higher heights. He was involved in all aspects of school life from gardening to graduation. Towards the end of his life he mortgaged his home to support some worthy school project. STATHS was his life, and as fate would have it, he died on the job at school in the summer of 1990.

I can't express my gratitude enough to my early mentors, who have helped in moulding my outlook on life and have prepared me for the valleys that lay ahead along life's treacherous journey.

But there were moments of relief and joy, and one such moment was when I encountered romance in the valley.

L-R: Beres, Derrick, Papa, Flo, Sherrill (cousin), Maxine - 1954

Left
*Flo
University of
the West Indies
1964*

Right
*Trevor
Age 19 years*

31 White Hall Avenue - 1965
L-R (Back to front row): Papa, Flo, Maxine, Cris, Karl, Mama, Karlene, Patty, Paul, Mike

Spaulding, Manchester - 1967
L-R: Flo, Karlene, Mike, Karl, Papa

Diamonds are excellent conductors of heat

2

ROMANCE IN THE VALLEY

Bev

Henry Street in Port of Spain on the island of Trinidad seemed particularly busy that morning as we hurried towards South Quay. The Feast of Tabernacles 1974 was on its way. It was held during the first week of October, and arrangements were made for a shuttle maxi-taxi to transport feastgoers from South Quay to Chacacabana hotel, the feast site.

It was our inaugural feast in Trinidad and Tobago. Mommy and I were excited and wanted to be there on time. We were late as we approached the pick-up area. What appeared to be the last shuttle was about to leave and its last passenger about to board. He got on board just before we arrived. Unfortunately, there was only one seat left in the maxi.

Disappointedly, we realized that if this were indeed the last shuttle maxi, then we would have to make some alternative arrangements quickly. As we turned away, a deep but gentle voice called out to us, "Would you like to have my seat?" I looked around to see the last passenger to board disembarking. He smiled warmly and motioned us towards the door. He was tall, about six feet, of light brown complexion with a full beard. He was dressed in a dark blue pants and a cream long-sleeve shirt, with a bible and a notebook in his left hand. There was just enough space left in the maxi for Mommy and I. The maxi sped off towards the Diego Martin main road. I looked back to see this stranger waving goodbye as we embarked on our trip to Chacacabana. I gave a three-finger wave back to him.

My thoughts went back in time two years before when I was 14 years old and my parents separated. I had lived in Pleasantville, San Fernando all my life. My parents began having problems getting along. Daddy was not a communicator, and he was alcoholic, so Mommy felt more and more isolated. Matters between them came to a head in 1972 when she said she could no longer take the distress that followed when Daddy came home from one of his drinking sessions. She decided that in our best interest we would move and live with her sister Ena in Port of Spain. Auntie was happy to accommodate us under the circumstances.

It is never easy when parents separate, so when we left Pleasantville, San Fernando that morning, Daddy stood on the front porch and waved goodbye. I waved back, and that was the last I saw of him for many months.

We had arrived at the Chacacabana Hotel during the day. Mommy and I looked for the stranger and we found him in the company of a Jamaican U.W.I. student, Cleveland, who had recently joined our church. Mommy expressed our thanks to him and he warmly smiled back with the words "No problem!" He introduced himself as Michael. He and his friend were studying Engineering. His accent and voice sounded jokey, I thought to myself.

Time passed quickly, and soon it was announced in church that Michael Case, affectionately called Mike, had completed his studies and was heading back to Jamaica. We were not particularly close during those months, as I was too busy studying for my GCE exams, and he also was too busy studying for his final exams at the University.

However, after this final church service, he approached me with a list that could have been close to 30 names and addresses and asked if I could add my name and address to the list. He wanted to keep in touch. I gladly obliged.

Over the next year we corresponded. I particularly enjoyed his sense of humor, as he would tell me stories of his childhood and his future plans. I started looking forward to receiving his letters; by then he told me that all the other 30 persons had stopped writing. I had enjoyed reading and writing since I was a little girl attending primary school, so I enjoyed corresponding with him. Mike had a gifting for poetry. I was delighted when he wrote special poems about our friendship and what it meant to him.

"I was in no position to become too serious about settling down"

In February of 1976, Mike on his return from a working visit to Guyana, stopped off for a few days in Trinidad and Tobago and so we spent some time together. It was during this time I realised how attracted I was to him. However, I was in no position to become too serious about settling down. Mike was five years my senior and though he may have been ready for marriage, I just had too many plans ahead of me.

My aunt Carmen, Mommy's eldest sister, had filed for us to obtain landed immigrant status in Canada. I was looking forward to that and to furthering my tertiary education. I liked journalism but also wanted to do something involving children; so I thought that I would be writing children's books.

I was not the only one who fell for Mike. Mommy, who had always wanted a son, had her eyes on him for me.

There was a period of time when Mike and I had stopped corresponding for months. A misunderstanding of correspondence protocol, added to the fact that I felt I needed more time to evaluate my options, led to a drought of interaction between us from early 1976 until about September of that year. Mike later confided to me that he had thought he had lost me after my good friend Cheryl wrote him advising him that what he was suffering from was a case of unrequited love and that he should move on and forget about me.

Thankfully, that impasse did not last forever, and after we resumed writing, the tone of Mike's letters took a deeper, more romantic flavour.

By September of that year Daddy became ill in San Fernando. When we visited him in the hospital, he was in a diabetic coma and was unable to recognize us. Daddy had also suffered much damage to his liver as a result of his heavy drinking habits.

He died without regaining consciousness a few days before the Feast of Tabernacles in 1976. When he died I called Mike, who tried to change his plans and come for the funeral, but there was an airline strike that crippled all flights in and out of Trinidad and Tobago. It wasn't until the day after the funeral that he turned up. I started feeling remorseful and grief stricken over Daddy's death. He had a disease called alcoholism that none of us really understood, so he was probably denied the counselling and treatment that he needed to deal effectively with this situation.

After the Feast had ended, Mike stayed back in Trinidad for a few days. We spent most of the time together. I really enjoyed talking with Mike. He had such a tender heart, and since Daddy's sickness and death I needed someone to talk with, someone who could really empathise with and understand my feelings. I believe it was at this time that romance really flourished. On the night before he departed for Jamaica, he visited. Both of us sat together in the front room in each other's embrace, sharing some very special moments. The light was dim and the radio station started playing ballads from the early seventies, the Chilites and Stylistics; they were among our favourites.

> **"Mike did not make a formal proposal, but we both knew we wanted to get married to each other"**

We got up and Mike held me in his arms, and we started dancing. Mike did not make a formal proposal, but we both knew we wanted to get married to each other. Mike was six feet, and I was just over five feet; we danced slowly across the living room. He told me how much he loved me and promised that he would always be there for me for better or for worse, in sickness and in health. He promised to be a good father to our children; he ended by saying these special words: "Bev, I love you more than I love myself." He then reached down and we kissed. I felt so warm, so secure in the loving arms of this gentle giant.

My father was taken from me by death, but God had provided a father, a brother and a best friend all in one person, my beloved Mike.

Mike left the following morning for Jamaica. The days, weeks and months seemed to have flown by and soon in December Mike was back, this time with an engagement ring, which he presented to me soon after arriving. He asked Mommy for her blessing and got it. Mommy had always liked Mike since that first day at the maxi-taxi stop at South Quay.

The big day arrived, Sunday March 6, 1977. I was still on cloud nine and thought to myself that I must be the most blessed young lady on the planet. I am getting married today to my best friend, I thought to myself. Mike's brother, Beres, was his best man and one of his sisters, Patty, was one of my bridesmaids. It was like real magic as Uncle Frank, Mommy's eldest brother, walked me up the aisle to the instrumental sounds of Ludwig Van Beethoven's Romance, to meet, waiting at the altar, my Prince Charming.

Normally in our church it was not advisable, nor was it the custom, for members to marry before age 20. I was in my nineteenth year, and Mr Gordon Harry, our Minister, thought that despite our ages we were both mature enough to know what we were getting into. He had offered us much pre-marital counselling.

I wore an empire line gown made with a high neckline and arm- length sleeves richly appliqued with Swiss embroidered guipure lace motifs. The gown featured a detachable cathedral train also appliqued with the guipure flowers. Gloves, a bouquet of contrasting red carnations and three-tiered veil completed the design. The bridesmaids, all five of them, were attired in a fawn sleeveless ankle length four-tiered dress. The groomsmen wore matching colored kareba suits.

The wedding went smoothly and, unlike most young brides, I was not nervous. I was getting married to my best friend. We had spent hours together sharing our thoughts, hopes, dreams and aspirations; so I knew what lay ahead, and I knew that he was honest and sincere.

As I approached the altar, Mike turned around and smiled with that familiar warm smile that I had become accustomed to. Mike was impeccably attired in a light blue three-piece suit with a matching necktie. He turned around and received me from Uncle Frank. It was a real magical moment. I smiled and breathed a sigh of relief when the Minister, Mr Harry, said, "I now pronounce you husband and wife." I felt a moment of sorrow for Mike, whose parents were unable to share this moment with us. He always spoke highly of his parents, so highly that I knew he too was disappointed. In our haste, we had not given enough notice for them to make preparations to attend.

We honeymooned at the Chacacabana Hotel, the site where we were first introduced to each other. I have always said that God made us for each other, and I thank him every day of my life for the same gentle giant and "Prince Charming" that he gave me. After 35 years, we are now more in love than we ever were. If I had to do it all over again, I would be back at South Quay waiting for the same warm friend, so we may journey together into the sunset.

Wedding Day
Port of Spain, Trinidad - March 1977

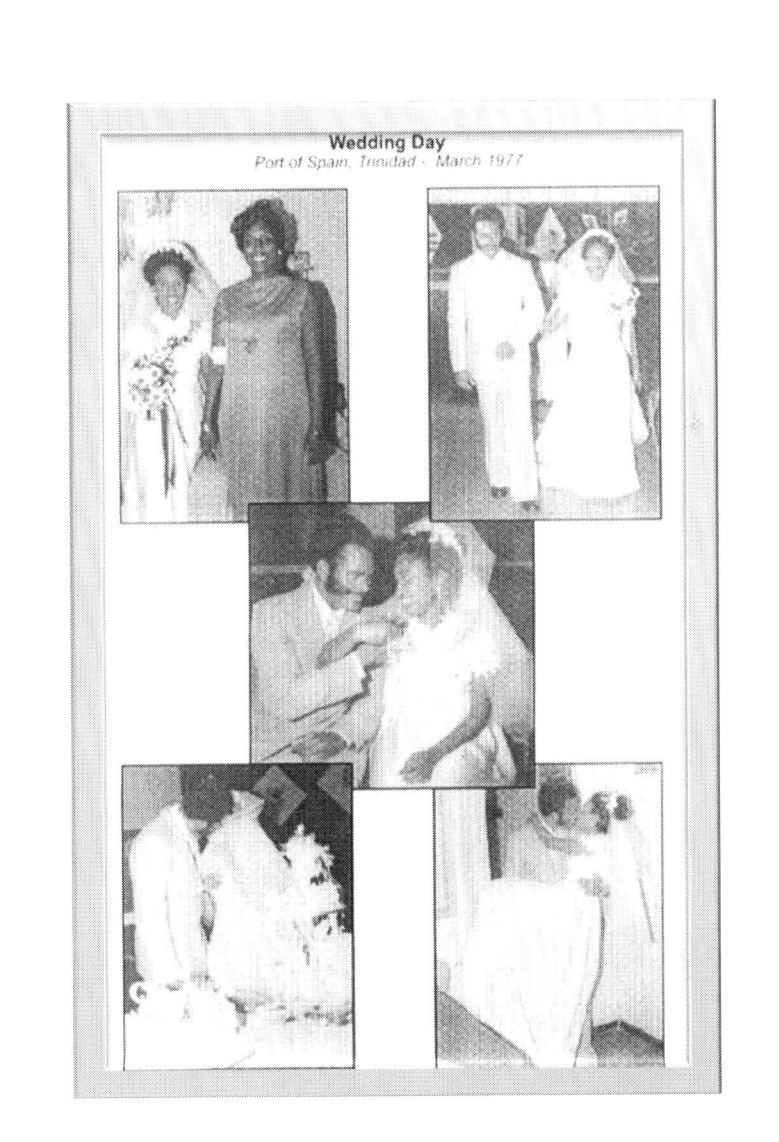

Over 80 percent of diamonds are of low quality suitable for use in industrial abrasive.

3

LESSONS IN THE VALLEY

Mike and Bev
A benefit of valley experiences is the opportunity it affords to build Godly character and compassion. This is God's purpose for human beings from the beginning.
Let us make man in our Image, in our Likeness.
Genesis 1:26

God has never deviated from His overall purpose of reproducing Himself in man. God made man after the God kind, and today He desires that we be fashioned after the image of the stature of the fullness of Christ as illuminated by the Apostle Paul in the book of Ephesians chapter 4. Can you grasp the significance of this truth? The Apostle Paul wrote:
And not only so, but we glory in tribulations also, knowing that tribulation worketh patience; And patience, experience; and experience hope; And hope maketh not ashamed, because the love of God is shed abroad in our Hearts by the Holy Spirit who is given unto us.
Romans 5:3 - 5 (KJV)

The word "experience" in the text is derived from the original Greek word meaning "character." Godly character therefore, involves a wilful commitment to do what is right regardless of the consequences. Therefore by virtue of the definition of character and the need for process, it is not something that God does instantly by fiat. Where humans are involved, time is necessary. God, in fashioning mankind after the God kind, is building in him His righteous character, and this is done through the vehicle of trial, testing and suffering.

James, the Lord's brother, in his letter wrote:

Consider it pure joy my brothers whenever you face trials of many kinds, because you know that the testing of your faith develops perseverance. Perseverance must finish its work so that you may be mature and complete, not lacking anything.

James 1:2 - 4

Here again the concept of spiritual maturity is linked to perseverance, or patient endurance, which is one of the ingredients of building the image of God's own character in us. The phrase "trials of many kinds" or "divers temptation" (KJV) in the original Greek language suggests many colors, as of a spectrum.

It is interesting to note that as steel is heated in a furnace or converter, it goes through color changes at different temperatures. The greater the temperature, the greater levels of purification and refinement that occurs as follows:

Approximate Temperature (°C) vs. Color of Steel:
550 - Dull red
800 - Cherry red
1000 - Orange
1100 - Yellow
1300 – Yellow-white
1400 - White

This is reminiscent of the passage in the book of Daniel, where it states:

Many shall be purified, and made white, and tested.

Daniel 12:10

Pig Iron, the most impure form of iron, is produced and refined in a furnace; as the iron-ore melts; the slag or impurities rise to the top and are skimmed off by the furnace operator.

Steel in its original state is of comparatively little value and use, but when subjected to certain heat treatment processes such as annealing, normalising, hardening and tempering, it can be put to almost limitless uses in industry and the home. In a similar manner as the heat of trials and testing is turned up on us, the impurities and flaws in our character are brought to the top where they can be exposed, identified and 'skimmed' off in a process of confession, repentance and forsaking. Then and only then can we be prepared and available for the limitless range of service to humanity.

"God is in the process of refining our character in life's valleys of testing"

The proverb "Iron sharpens Iron" presupposes that the iron is hardened and tempered by heat, without which sharpening would be an impossible feat. The Apostle Peter in his first epistle picks up on the same thought:

In this you greatly rejoice though now for a while you may have had to suffer grief in all kinds of trials. These have come so that your faith – of greater worth than gold, which perishes even though refined by fire – may be proved genuine and may result in praise, glory and honour when Jesus Christ is revealed.
1 Peter 1:6 - 7

Peter compares our faith to being more precious than gold. God, in the book of Malachi, also refers to His people as His jewels. Gold and other precious metals like silver are always mined in a valley, not on a mountaintop. Diamonds are the most valuable of precious stones. Diamonds are formed when graphite, which is actually a rather common substance, is subjected to years of intense heat and pressure; the greater the heat and pressure and the deeper the valley, the more precious the diamond.

God is in the process of refining our character in life's valleys of testing. Peter further developed this thought by addressing the concept of unjust suffering in his first epistle, the second chapter; he admonishes us when we suffer unjustly not to retaliate but to commit everything to God who judges justly. We must look to Christ who suffered unjustly and committed Himself to God in the process.

According to the Apostle Peter, there is a victory that comes from suffering patiently and unjustly:

Therefore, since Christ suffered in his body, arm yourselves also with the same attitude, because he who has suffered in his body is done with sin. As a result, he does not live the rest of his earthly life for evil human desires, but rather for the will of God.
1 Peter 4:1 - 2

The point being made here is that sin loses its hold on us when we suffer patiently and with perseverance. We must keep our eyes on Christ and commit ourselves to God who judges justly because in the process we are building the very character of God, which is pure, and righteous. Peter further illuminates the process in chapter 4. He admonishes us not to be surprised at the fiery trials as something strange. In other words, these trials are to be expected. The Apostle Paul takes the same concept and builds even further on it in book of Philippians chapter 3. In verses 4-9 Paul lists his earthly credentials, which he then considered as nothing. Paul writes:

I want to know Christ and the power of his resurrection and the fellowship of sharing his sufferings, becoming like him in his death, and so, somehow, to attain to the resurrection from the dead.
Philippians 3:10 - 11

Paul's life quest was to intimately know Christ, including the fellowship of sharing in His suffering. This fellowship builds bonds.

> **"The only qualities that are preserved beyond the grave are the spiritual, not the physical or material."**

We cannot attain to resurrection power unless God proves us in suffering and in the crucifixion death of our fleshly lusts. There are simply no short cuts to building God's character in us and fulfilling His purposes for our lives, even if it means that we have to go the route of the saints of old who had a clearer understanding of the role of suffering in their lives than we do today in our instant society.

In the second book of Corinthians chapter 11, Paul lists his various modes of suffering as credentials for his apostolic office when his apostleship was questioned by some at Corinth. Some of these included; imprisonment, flogging, stoning, cold and nakedness, shipwrecking, in danger from bandits at sea, hunger, thirst, and the concerns and failures of the brethren under his care. In chapter 12 verse 1-10, Paul explains that because of the abundance of the revelation he had, God had given him a thorn in the flesh to keep him humble. This Paul accepted:

That is why for Christ's sake, I delight in weakness, in insults, in hardships, in persecutions, in difficulties. For when I am weak then, I am strong.
2 Corinthians 12:10

One of the most encouraging passages of scripture in this context is the book of Hebrews chapter 11, often called the Faith Chapter. Here we have listed some of the giants of the faith who have blazed trails down through the ages; those who have had their 'pictures hung' in the "Hall of Faith" of His glory:

And what more shall I say? I do not have time to tell about Gideon, Barak, Samson, Jephthah, David, Samuel, and the prophets, who through faith conquered kingdoms, administered justice and gained what was promised; who shut the mouths of lions, quenched the fury of the flames, and escaped the edge of the sword; whose weakness was turned to strength, and who became powerful in battle and routed foreign armies. Women received back their dead, raised to life again. Others were tortured and refused to be released, so that they might gain a better resurrection. Some faced jeers and flogging, while still others were chained and put in prison. They were stoned; they were sawed in two; they were put to death by the sword. They went about in sheepskins and goatskins, destitute,

> *persecuted and mistreated - the world was not worthy of them. They wandered in deserts and mountains, and in caves and holes in the ground.*
> *Hebrews 11:32 - 38*

God sees our potential, and if we were given the talents to be twenty karat gold jewel and we are only operating at fourteen karats, then God allows further purification in the valley to bring out the additional six karats. This is because the only qualities that are preserved beyond the grave are the spiritual, not the physical or material. So, a loving Father will often allow us to go through valley after valley to mine the additional karats for eternity.

The average life expectancy in the West is, let's say, seventy years. How does one really compare this three score and ten years with eternity? God gave us this present existence to prepare us for real life in His glory. Most of us know what a thousand years are; It's represented by; one, followed by three zeros. A million is represented by; one followed by six zeros. A billion is represented by; one followed by nine zeros. Try to picture the time span represented by; one followed by a billion zeros. If you can conceptualise that in years then you would not have even scratched the surface of eternity. That is what God has destined for us. My friends, let's not short-change our eternity by putting an undue emphasis on the physical, material things of this three score and ten years. God wants us to attain our maximum potential and not to fall short of stars in our crown of glory. God is not as interested in giving us a Rolls Royce car in this life as he is in building within us a Rolls Royce quality character.

"Jesus is our compassionate high priest because of the obedient suffering He endured"

Another quality that is built by valley experiences is compassion. In the book of Hebrews, the author explains:
> *Therefore, since we have a great high priest who has gone through the heavens, Jesus the Son of*

God, let us hold firmly to the faith we profess. For we do not have a high priest who is unable to sympathize with our weaknesses, but we have one who has been tempted in every way, just as we are — yet was without sin. Let us then approach the throne of grace with confidence, so that we may receive mercy and find grace to help us in our time of need
Hebrews 4:14 - 16

Also in the same book we read:
During the days of Jesus' life on earth, he offered up prayers and petitions with loud cries and tears to the one who could save him from death, and he was heard because of his reverent submission. Although he was a son, he learned obedience from what he suffered and, once made perfect, he became the source of our eternal salvation for all who obey him.
Hebrews 5:7 - 10

Jesus is our compassionate high priest because of the obedient suffering He endured, so too we, unless we have suffered, cannot truly empathize with others in their suffering. Very often before Christ healed someone the narrative would say:

And Jesus was moved with compassion, and healed.

It's often out of our compassion for the sick that the healing virtue of God flows. Those of us in an intercessory or hospital ministry, often need to have spent some time in a hospital bed ourselves, so we can identify with the suffering of others, out of which compassion, and hence healing, will flow.

Paul writes, in the second book of Corinthians chapter 1, verse 3 that we are able to comfort others based on the comfort we have received from God. Very often God uses a person in a ministry capacity where he or she has suffered and received some level of comfort. God's objective here is His love flowing through us to others.

In the first book of Corinthians Paul writes:
No temptation has seized you except what is common to man. And God is faithful; he will not let you be tempted beyond what you can bear. But when you are tempted, he will also provide a way out so that you can stand up under it.
1 Corinthians 10:13

This is a very comforting truth for those trusting Him. We all face similar valleys in life, but through it all we can be comforted in knowing that help is available and that God, in the book of Hebrews chapter 13, has promised to those who trust Him, that He will never leave nor forsake them.

Staying on track is important, and this is yet another benefit of valley experiences. Imagine taking a flight from Kingston, Jamaica to London, England and the pilot sets a course that is one degree off-track. Normally, one degree when viewed at the circumference of a standard protractor subtends an arc of no more than one millimetre.

However, if that airline pilot maintains that off-course track and does not make any correction, by the time he touches down approximately 10,000 kilometres away, he would have missed his mark by over 150 kilometres or approximately 90 miles. Being that far off course, he would probably crash into the sea.

We must stay on the course that God has set. But our human tendency is to veer from the prescribed course set by a wise and loving God. In order to bring us back, God has to apply some mid-course corrections or discipline.

In this regard the history of God's dealings with the children of Israel is instructive. The history of Israel may be accurately described as cyclical. A spiritual high is followed by disobedience, then punishment, then repentance, then restoration, then disobedience, and so on, repeated throughout Israel's history.

Usually, the prophets were God's messengers to a disobedient Israel. For example, at the time of the divided kingdom, Jeremiah was a prophet sent specifically to the house of Judah, when Israel was in the disobedience phase of their cycle.

In Jeremiah we read:

This is the word that came to Jeremiah from the Lord: Go down to the potter's house, and there I will give you my message. So I went down to the potter's house, and I saw him working at the wheel. But the pot he was shaping from the clay was marred in his hands; so the potter formed it into another pot shaping it as seemed best to him. Then the word of the Lord came to me: O house of Israel, can I not do with you as this potter does? declares the Lord. Like clay in the hand of the potter, so are you in my hand, O house of Israel. If at any time I announce that a nation or kingdom is to be uprooted, torn down and destroyed, and if that nation I warned repents of evil, then I will relent and not inflict on it the disaster I had planned. And if at another time I announce that a nation or kingdom is to be built up and planted, and if it does evil in my sight and does not obey me, then I will reconsider the good I had intended to do for it. Now therefore say to the people of Judah and those living in Jerusalem, this is what the Lord says: Look! I am preparing a disaster for you and devising a plan against you. So turn from your evil ways, each one of you, and reform your ways and your actions. But they will reply, It's no use. We will continue with our own plans; each of us will follow the stubbornness of his evil heart.
Jeremiah 18:1 - 12

The Lord likens Himself to the Master Potter, and we His subjects are the clay. To get a clearer insight into the lessons and observations of Jeremiah at the potter's house, we need to look at the steps taken by the potter in forming pottery from raw clay.

First, the potter selects the clay. Similarly, God selects us. We are referred to as a chosen generation and a royal priesthood in the first book of Peter chapter 2. Each one of us is a unique specimen, individually fashioned by God.

Different qualities of clay are used for different purposes; so in the body of Christ we are many members but the same body, as explained in the first book of Corinthians chapter 12. Our functions will be different in the same way that our bodily members have different roles to perform.

Second, after selecting the clay the potter next begins to beat out the lumps; this is accomplished by a rod designed to inflict heavy blows on the clay to smash these lumps. Similarly the human character is flawed with many lumps like, pride, vanity, arrogance, and selfishness to name a few, and God's discipline will smash these lumps to much smaller pebbles.

Third, the potter then adds oil and water and begins to massage the clay with his hands to dissolve the pebbly lumps that remain; this way the clay becomes pliable, malleable and easy to work with. It can now be formed into whatever image the potter desires. Oil and water are symbolic of God's Holy Spirit.

"God adds to us His precious Holy Spirit so we can become more pliable in His hands"

God adds to us His precious Holy Spirit so we can become more pliable in His hands; so he can fashion us into the stature of the fullness of Christ. The Holy Spirit is added to us not just so that we can speak in tongues or perform miracles, but so that we can relate to and get along with our neighbors.

Afterwards, the potter puts the clay on his potter's wheel. Then, as the wheel turns, the potter uses both hands to mould the pottery into the desired shape. This process goes on until the final touches are completed and the pottery has now taken shape according to the desired purpose. If you ever felt like you were going around in circles, then maybe, just maybe, you were being spun on the Master Potter's wheel!

In the final stage of this process, the potter puts the pottery into the oven and turns up the heat. The potter wants to make sure that having spun the clay into his desired shape, it can now be permanent and hard, so the heat is turned up to glaze the pottery. Different pottery for different purposes requires different levels of heat; so don't be surprised if the heat turned up on your colleague is less than yours. The chances are that your purpose is one of a higher or different calling than your colleague. When the pottery is taken out of the oven, it is now ready to fulfil its purpose, not before. Jeremiah, one of the great prophets, has left this analogy, the pattern that we can always use to better understand God's working among and in us.

The story of the prophets Isaiah, Ezekiel and Hosea, all teach us that God orchestrates events in the lives of His prophets to picture the spiritual state of Israel and Judah as He was married to them and called upon them to repent or face His discipline.

Isaiah was another prophet sent by God to warn the nation of Judah of its wayward ways before correcting them. God had Isaiah walk through the streets of the cities with his buttocks uncovered to picture the shameful condition of the state of the nation of Judah, this is recorded in the 20th chapter of Isaiah.

Ezekiel prophesied both to Judah and Israel, and God had this prophet lie on both sides of his body in turn, in the streets of the city, for a period of over four hundred days. The experience was used to prophesy the impending doom and captivity of both nations, as recorded in Ezekiel chapter 4.

God commissioned Hosea to the nation of Israel. God had ordered him to marry a woman of harlotry who eventually became unfaithful to him, as recorded in Hosea chapter one. All of this was to picture the unfaithfulness of the nation of Israel who Jeremiah in his book, the third chapter described as God's wife. The lives of these holy men of God were hardly enviable.

Both nations after failing to heed repeated divine warnings were led into captivity; Israel in 722 BC by the Assyrians and Judah in 586 BC by the Babylonians. God's warnings and discipline are for our eternal good. In Hebrews, the writer further develops the thought of God's discipline:

In your struggle against sin you have not yet resisted to the point of shedding your blood. And you have forgotten that word of encouragement

that addresses you as sons: My son, do not make light of the Lord's discipline, and do not lose heart when he rebukes you, because the Lord disciplines those he loves, and he punishes everyone he accepts as a son. Endure hardship as discipline; God is treating you as sons. For what son is not disciplined by his father? If you are not disciplined (and everyone undergoes discipline), then you are illegitimate children and not true sons. Moreover, we have all had human fathers who disciplined us and we respected them for it. How much more should we submit to the Father of our spirits and live! Our fathers disciplined us for a little while as they thought best; but God disciplines us for our good, that we may share in his holiness. No discipline seems pleasant at the time, but painful. Later on, however, it produces a harvest of righteousness and peace for those who have been trained by it.
Hebrews 12:4 - 11

As the writer of Hebrews says, the discipline is painful, but it is for our good, because if we endure it we will afterwards enjoy an abundance of righteousness and peace.

Phyllis
(Adopted sister) 1965

Left
Beres
White Hall Ave.
1966

Right
Mike
Age 17

White Hall Avenue - 1968
L-R (Back to front row): Ricky, Micky,
Beres, Maxine, Papa, Mama, Trevor,
Shannette, Cherry, Derrick, Mike,
Karlene, Karl, Patty, Cris, Paul.

White Hall Avenue - 1969
L-R: Patty, Cris, Karl, Karlene, Maxine,
Flo, Papa, Mama, Trevor, Paul, Mike

Natural diamonds are formed deep in the earth's interior, at least 90 miles from the surface, where conditions of extreme heat and pressure work together to squeeze carbon atoms into the diamonds compact crystalline structure

4

PHILIP IN THE VALLEY

Mike

The word of God is silent on the emotions and feelings of God the Father on the suffering and death of His one and only son, Jesus. Yet, we realize that God is capable of laughter, anger, remorse, disappointment, love, hate and tears... yes, tears.

We want to share a period in our lives that has brought us much laughter and at the same time much tears.

Immediately after our honeymoon we returned to Jamaica to live. I was then working at the Ministry of Agriculture as a Junior Engineer. Our first child, Michael Antony Jr., arrived a year later, on Sunday morning January 15, amidst much excitement and celebration. (So much for our plans to wait two years before starting a family!)

By the beginning of the following year the second child was on the way. There was much excitement and expectation that a playmate would be on the way for Mike Jr., a baby brother or sister. We decided, as we did before when Mike Jr. arrived, that a delivery at home with the same mid-wife and me assisting would be the appropriate way to go.

On Saturday September 1, 1979 at about 10 p.m., while visiting Opal, a friend and a long time church sister in Kingston, Bev felt an extreme pressure on her pelvic region. Within a half hour her amniotic sac was ruptured and we realised that she had entered premature labor, as this child was not due until the end of the month. A Nigerian doctor who was close by examined her and advised us to proceed with plans for delivery.

At the time we were living in Maryland, a few miles up the Gordon Town Road and too far to go back. We decided to rush to Don and Alice Roach's residence in Hope Pastures, who themselves had recently borne twins at home.

While being helped into the house, Bev felt the baby's head crowning and cried out. Within two hours of her first sign of labor, Philip Stuart came gushing out in the back seat of the car in the Roach's driveway.

Bev was later taken by our good friend Cleveland to the University Hospital ward where Philip was registered and attended. Don Roach and I meanwhile drove to August Town in search of our Midwife, Nurse Sinclair. Philip weighed 5 ½ lbs. He was hairy, long and rosy red in complexion.

"Philip was a bundle of joy to have around. He was the perfect playmate for Mike Jr"

Philip was a bundle of joy to have around. He was the perfect playmate for Mike Jr. Whenever he was missed, he would be most likely found somewhere inside the floor kitchen cupboards, with a spoon in one hand, a pot over his head, and a broad smile on his face. Time seems to have flown, and soon little Philip was walking around and muttering a few words like "dada". He was by this time sixteen months old.

But his life of youthful joy was not to last. Permit us to share an experience we had late 1980 to early 1981. After a day of fever and occasional stiffness in his limbs, Philip was diagnosed with the deadly disease, meningitis.

This is a disease that is contracted sometimes through a common cold; the virus then attacks the spinal column and leads to enlargement of the brain. In its worst state it can lead to a child wasting away, static pneumonia and often death. Philip was hospitalised in late November and spent close to six weeks on ward 16, at the University of the West Indies Hospital, Mona.

The entire ordeal lasted forty days, to be exact. On the morning of January 7, 1981 we visited him as we did every day of his hospitalisation. On this day, however, Philip was obviously wasting away. He was barely skin and bones, breathing was difficult and labored. Philip in the final days of his ordeal had contracted static pneumonia. This was as a result of his inability to move around and his stupefied condition, both due to the medication he was on and his deteriorating condition.

On that morning it was difficult, to say the least, for both of us to stand there helplessly witnessing him deteriorating. At about 10 a.m. Philip suffered a cardiac arrest. We had noticed that his labored breathing had ceased, that he was no longer "heaving and hoeing" and was lifeless as a log. We alerted the medical staff on the ward, who summoned a consultant. It was then that we realised what had happened. Philip's tiny heart was unable to labor on its own any longer and had failed. His heart and lungs ceased to operate and if left unattended would die in a matter of minutes. Within seconds there was a scurry of activities on the ward as doctors, nurses and other attendants darted around to his aid.

It was as if time had stood still and all creation was zeroed in on the life of one little sixteen-month old boy. Machines, needles and drugs were brought to the scene as they all converged around his bed. I can clearly remember as if it happened yesterday. The consultant paediatrician, a rather polite mature woman, motioned to my wife and me that we had to turn away while the physicians and nurses put all their energies into saving the life of our little boy.

"The Lord took me back in time to Calvary where two thousand years ago another father had turned his back on his dying son"

Satan sometimes is allowed to attack our children or us, but God always turns the worst of all seeming disasters into lessons, benefits and eventual blessings for His people. Satan viciously attacked our little boy, but God in His infinite wisdom turned it around into what proved to be a once in a lifetime experience.

As I turned my back and looked away from Philip's bed that morning, the Lord took me back in time to Calvary where two thousand years ago another father had turned his back on his dying son. I never understood it then, and even though in a limited way shared it with those who were our spiritual leaders at the time, we didn't until more recent years appreciate the lessons that God the Father was teaching us.

It is possible to study the Bible for a lifetime and not understand some things. There are levels in God that He Himself has to walk you through, and no reading will give you what experience in the valley can teach you. I felt as if God was reaching out to me at a level I have never had before. It's as if He took off His shoes, pointed to them and said, "Son, occupy these for a moment in time."

I remember feeling somewhat helpless and numb, but that morning, in spirit, I caught a rare glimpse of what God the Father's face looked like when He turned His back on His dying son. I saw tears, from an all-loving Dad who was in deep distress at the loss of fellowship with His one and only Son.

Philip revived for a while but expired later that night, shortly after we had returned home from visiting him. I remember early the next morning, Thursday, January 8, waking up to see our assistant pastor and his wife at our front door. We knew instinctively that they had brought news of Philip's death. The hospital had called them and asked that they give us the news. Both of them and the entire local church family were like towers of strength to us during this testing period of our lives.

His wife remained home with Bev that morning while he and I went to the hospital morgue. I wanted to see Philip. To me he was not just a body or a number in a refrigerator cell, but our own son. The morgue attendant drew out the tray with his linen wrapped body and unveiled his face.

No one knows the agony and pain at the loss of a child until one experiences this loss. I couldn't hold back the tears, and I remembered muttering in a low tone,

Oh Philip, you came to us in a hurry, and my God, you left us in a greater hurry.

I still recall some of what God was teaching us about Himself. I would have done anything to see Philip live, including giving him my own heart.

When I had to turn away from him, I had not much of a choice. God had a choice; He could have summoned legions of angels and released Christ at any moment. But for our good, yes, for our eternal good, He chose not to. The doctors and nurses who surrounded Philip as he struggled to live were all working for his good to see him revived and be given a chance at life. The evil beings that surrounded God's only Son Jesus on the Cross were enemies trying their level best to derail Him and finish Him off in utter shame.

Our son Philip died that night under the watchful care of doctors, nurses and attendants. God's only Son, Jesus, died totally alone with no one assisting Him in any way. It was indeed a bitter pill to swallow. Philip's forty-day ordeal; November 29 to January 7, came to an end, and we both look forward to being with him one day and to once again hold him close to us.

It was a tough way to learn lessons, but through it all God has drawn us into some experiential understanding of Himself that is priceless. We cherish Philip's memory each year as we prepare for the Passover observance, for now we have an added dimension to our understanding of His Passion, because of our little Philip.

We dedicate this chapter to the memory of Philip, whose life was cut short, but through whose death a greater light now shines in our lives.

Praise and glory be to God the most High.

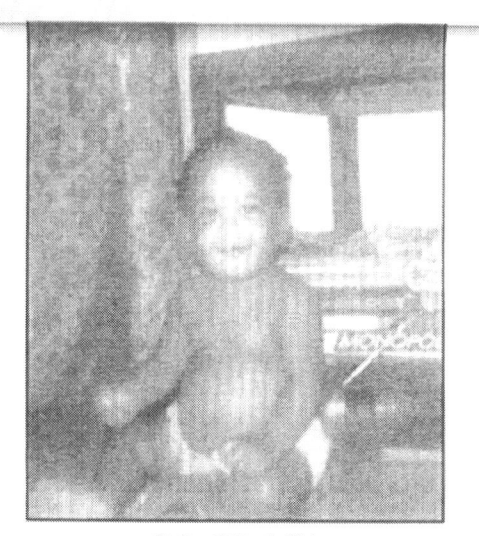

Philip - 7 Month Old
Maryland, St. Andrew

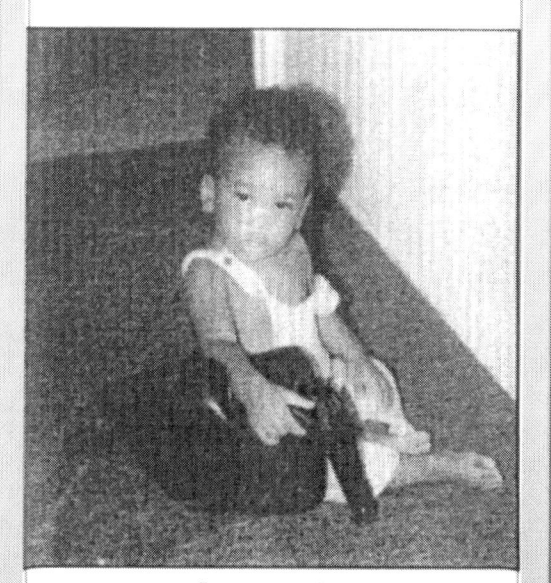

Philip - 1 Year Old
Runaway Bay, St. Ann

Rough Diamonds

On the basis of their macroscopic properties it seems improbable that diamonds and graphite are made of exactly the same atoms

5

BANDITS IN THE VALLEY

Mike

Philip's death had left a void in our lives. Michael Jr., our firstborn son, was not yet three when Philip died. We were living in a quiet residential area in the suburbs of St. Andrew, in Jamaica. The impact of Philip's loss was evident even in Mike Jr.'s life. Philip was a blessing to us from God as a brother and playmate for him.

To relieve the pain of our loss, we got more involved in church activities. At this time our church was producing a musical drama entitled, "Esther"; a story of a beautiful Jewish girl who became Queen in the Medio-Persian Empire and rescued her people from what seemed sure extinction. Bev acted the part of Esther and I was the king. On the morning of Sunday March 1, 1981, merely two months after Philip's death, we were preparing for a costume show at the church auditorium to follow within the week.

Our home was adjacent to an open lot with a large drain on the other side of the lot. I really was not comfortable with how the lot was positioned and situated. Our driveway was rather long, and we were located some distance on a curve away from the road. It was the only place available at the time, and since we needed somewhere to live, we took this place. We had neither a security system nor a dog for protection. Our neighbors, a middle aged couple, were within shouting distance from our back porch. We had only been living there four months when we had an unwelcome visitor.

We were making preparations for the upcoming costume show and were hardly aware that the living room door, although closed, was not locked. The bedrooms were down a passage midway the length of the living room, with the dining and kitchen area facing this passage.

Without our realizing it, someone had mounted the fence, crept through the front door unseen, and entered the house. At this time we were in Mike Jr's room, tidying up and getting costumes put aside. When I entered the living room by way of the passage, I was confronted with what seemed to be a nine-millimetre pistol pointed at my chest. The bandit behind the weapon could not have been more than eighteen years of age, short, dark, with a full face, pronounced features and low-cropped hair.

We were restrained and ordered to lie face down, but Mike Jr. was allowed to walk free of hindrance. It was then that I realised that there were more than one intruders, for I heard three distinct voices. There were three burglars in the house. I only had a good look at one of the faces. Robbery was their intent, and fortunately or unfortunately there was little or no cash in the house. For some time now we had been operating by check rather than cash, for this very same reason.

The thief with the deepest and roughest voice spoke first and demanded money. I felt helpless, for there was a size nine leather boot in my rib cage. I could not think clearly enough to answer coherently, so I paused awhile, and another impact was felt on the other side of my torso. I eventually got enough presence of mind to remember that Mike Jr.'s piggy bank was located on the left side of the chest of drawers in his room and directed them to it. They refused to accept such a small reward for their 'labors,' a jar of pennies, but indeed that was about the extent of the cash we had on hand.

I was planning to go to the bank the following day to withdraw the week's cash needs, so we were out of cash for that weekend. I heard the patter of Mike Jr's footsteps as he freely moved about in the house. I believe that he was too young to understand what was going on. Having witnessed Bev and me acting scenes from Esther, did he think to himself that this too must have been one of those scenes where the Jews were being persecuted? Who knows what was going through his little mind? I was unable to see or hear sounds from his direction, as Bev and I were shouted at repeatedly by the robbers.

I distinctly heard my own heartbeats and heavy breathing as I remained in somewhat of a frightened condition. These are the things that you read about happening to other people or perhaps what you see in movies, but it was as real as the palpitations of my heart.

It was about fifteen minutes into the ordeal. One burglar kept a keen eye out, while the other two took turns ransacking and turning every drawer, cabinet or dresser inside out and upside down in search of some money. It was then that I remembered to pray and said a quiet word of prayer calling on God to intervene. I wondered why it took me so long to get to this point, but in my frightened condition would not have been cognizant of the need to do anything but to wait it out. I asked God to protect us from harm and take us out safely, but I concluded, *"Whatever happens here, please take us safely into your kingdom together."*

"A towel was thrown over my head, and I waited for what I thought must now be the inevitable"

After about twenty minutes into the robbery, one of the perpetrators, obviously frustrated and desperate, shouted using expletives: "Shoot the man!!!" A whole barrage of expletives rang out from the third bandit. For possibly the first time in my life, I admit that I truly felt powerless and totally in God's hands. A towel was thrown over my head, and I waited for what I thought must now be the inevitable. It could not have taken more than a few moments, but it sure did seem like an eternity. So many thoughts raced through my mind. In a moment I thought, "Will Bev have to be a young widow, will they shoot her and Mike Jr. as well?"

This is where faith is really tested. I did not want to die, and in final desperation I cried out, "Lord Help!" There was an uneasy calm in the room. I could not see what was happening, but I guessed that an angel of God must have touched down. I recalled a passage of scripture that Papa would recite to us as children as we retired for the night:

The angel of the Lord encampeth round about those who fear him, and delivereth them.
Psalm 34:7 (KJV)

I do believe that one of these angels manifested himself in the living room, because just as I expected that I would have been shot in the head through the towel, one of the guys on his way out muttered something of the sort that they were now going. More calm pervaded for a minute. No sound, no shouting, no rustling of furniture drawers was heard. Mike Jr. came close, and I instructed him to pull me loose. He did so, and I pulled Bev loose.

We were still somewhat shaken as we looked around to see the mess created by these hoodlums. We took some time out to thank God for His intervention. My lower lip was cut from one of the blows I had received earlier, but apart from a sore rib cage and two trembling, shattered hearts, our lives were spared and we now had to pick up the pieces.

The thieves also made off with most of our jewellery, including our wedding and engagement bands, necklaces, chains, pendants, earrings and other heirloom items. We left the premises that same day and never returned.

We spent some time first with the Roaches then with Beres and his wife Marie and family, then with Maxine, her husband Micky and family, until we got some more permanent housing.

David wrote:
Though I walk through the valley of the shadow of death, I will fear no evil, for you are with me; your rod and your staff they comfort me.
Psalm 23:4

God allows us to tread these dark valleys at times so we can truly prove Him and His presence, and it would not have negated His love for us even if the worst had happened, because we would have been escorted into His glorious presence to abide with Him forever. God's truth never fails, and His love for us is eternal.

"Esther" Rehearsals - 1981

King Ahasuerus (Mike) Boasts of his Empire

King Ahasuerus receives report on Queen Vashti

Mordecai (Joe Brown) presents his niece Esther (Bev) for preparation to marry the King

Diamonds do not burn easily

6

A SOVEREIGN GOD IN THE VALLEY

Mike and Bev
Before time was, God is. And when time is ended God will be, for God is eternal without beginning and without end. There was in human terms, a time when there was no time. Then God created time to bring about a beginning in eternity's continuum.

God has existed from eternity in the past (before time) in three distinct personages or hypostases (Greek): God the Father, God the Word (later became Son) and God the Holy Spirit. They have always existed in perfect unity, harmony and true family, for God is one, a trinity in unity and a unity in trinity. God made human beings in His own image and likeness and so as a trinity or tri-partite being: spirit, soul and body. God's purpose for mankind, created in the image and likeness of God, involves living in unity with himself: spirit, soul and body and with others. By so doing we demonstrate the unity God desires.

There are some fundamental truths that we internalize, and these give us the strength to cope during times of severe testing. While Satan tempts us to destroy us, God tests us to strengthen us. There can be no more comforting truth than to know that our all-wise and all—loving Heavenly Father is supreme and sovereign. In view of this, we can be assured that when we go through painful experiences, He is with us and all that happens is part of a grand design and purpose by an all-wise and all-loving Sovereign God to fulfil His purpose in our lives.

The truth of this is clearly brought out in the book of the patriarch Job, arguably the oldest book of the Bible. Job, a wealthy and righteous man of the East was made to suffer to test his faithfulness to God. As the story goes, Satan asked God for permission to take away all of Job's possessions, including his family, in the hope that Job would turn against God.

The LORD said to Satan, Very well, then, everything he has is in your hands, but on the man himself do not lay a finger.
Job 1:12

Notice that God sets the bounds. Satan cannot do as he pleases. He cannot do anything unless God allows or gives him permission. Satan cannot oppress, suppress or cause a curse to come on you unless with the knowledge and permission of the Sovereign God of the universe. Satan evidently doesn't know the future and so he plays right into God's hands all the time. For example, he thought that he had killed the very Son of God. Little did he realise he was a puppet, an instrument in God's hands to bring redemption to all mankind. This is probably the most comforting truth anyone could understand.

God is sovereign and loving. He rules supreme; there is absolutely no competition between Him and the devil. Satan has to seek and obtain God's permission before he can inflict you with anything. Having failed in his attempt to tempt Job to curse God, Satan sought permission from God again, this time to inflict physical pain on Job's body.

Skin for skin! Satan replied. A man will give all he has for his own life. But stretch out your hand and strike his flesh and bones, and he will surely curse you to your face.
Job 2:4 - 5

The LORD said to Satan,
Very well then he is in your hands; but you must spare his life.
Job 2:5 - 6

Satan cannot take your life or the life of your loved ones unless he has God's permission. But a loving God watches us and will deal prudently with us. It is important to remember that God is total, selfless love. God never does anything except for our eternal good and welfare. If God allows suffering to come our way, then it is for our eternal good; even if He allows death to overtake our loved ones.

Precious in the sight of the LORD is the death of
his saints.
Psalm 116:15

We can relax, knowing that not even a sparrow can fall to the ground without God knowing or allowing it. If God takes the time to number the hairs on our heads, don't you think that He will watch out for our best interest?

> **"Nothing can take place in the universe without the knowledge and approval of the Sovereign God of all creation; this includes your life"**

The story of the book of Job ends on a happy note. Job's wealth, health and family were restored, and through the suffering he got to know God as sovereign. Then Job replied to the LORD:

I know that you can do all things; no plan of yours can be thwarted. You asked, who is this that obscures my counsel without knowledge? Surely I spoke of things I did not understand, things too wonderful for me to know. You said, Listen now and I will speak; I will question you, and you shall answer me! My ears had heard of you but now my eyes have seen you. Therefore I despise myself and repent in dust and ashes.
Job 42:1 - 6

Job learned of the sovereign nature of God. He also learned that God reserves the right to answer or not to answer our questions about why we suffer a particular trial. Nowhere in this account does it indicate that God told Job the reason for his severe suffering. God in His infinite wisdom knows best, and we have to trust His judgement in all things.

Nothing can take place in the universe without the knowledge and approval of the Sovereign God of all creation; this includes your life.

The story of the patriarch Joseph is another example of God's sovereign hand in the life of His people. When Joseph was at the tender age of seventeen, his ten brothers, moved by jealousies, sold him as a slave into Egypt. This may have seemed to be a very unjust act, but God in His sovereign power allowed it to take place. Then as an attendant in Potiphar's house, Joseph had so distinguished himself that Potiphar's entire trust was placed in his hands. The biblical account reads:

The LORD was with Joseph and he prospered and he lived in the house of his Egyptian master. When his master saw that the LORD was with him and that the LORD gave him success in everything he did, Joseph found favour in his eyes and became his attendant. Potiphar put him in charge of his household, and he entrusted to his care everything he owned. From the time he put him in charge of his household and of all that he owned, the LORD blessed the household of the Egyptian because of Joseph. The blessing of the Lord was on everything Potiphar had, both in the house and in the field. So he left in Joseph's care everything he had; with Joseph in charge, he did not concern himself with anything except the food he ate.
Genesis 39:2 - 6

Once again apparent misfortunes came Joseph's way. Potiphar's wife lusted after him, and after her advances were rejected she framed Joseph and had him put in prison. Once again, we ask what was Joseph's sin? He refused to do wrong and instead chose to do right. Of course, the Sovereign God of the universe is always watching and working out His purpose in our lives. Yet again Joseph distinguishes himself, this time in prison, and is put in charge of the other prisoners. Joseph's master took him and put him in prison, the place where the king's prisoners were confined.

But while Joseph was there in the prison, the LORD was with him: he showed him kindness and granted him favour in the eyes of the prison

warden. So the warden put Joseph in charge of all those held in the prison, and he was made responsible for all that was done there. The warden paid no attention to anything under Joseph's care, because the LORD was with Joseph and gave him success in whatever he did.
Genesis 39:20 - 23

After correctly interpreting the dreams of two of Pharaoh's servants who were cast into prison, Joseph reminded one of them to plead his case before Pharaoh because of his innocence, but he forgot about Joseph until two full years had passed, this is recorded in chapter 41.

Pharaoh had a dream and eventually summoned Joseph for an interpretation. Joseph was put over the entire operation of Egypt as second in command to Pharaoh.

So if you are tempted to ask why was this innocent young boy so viciously treated by his brothers and Potiphar's wife and forgotten in a jail cell by Pharaoh's servant - a total of thirteen long years of suffering - let Joseph, as he reveals his identity to his brothers, answer this question for himself: Joseph said his brothers,

I am Joseph! Is my father still living? But his brothers were not able to answer him, because they were terrified at his presence. Then Joseph said unto his brothers, come close to me. When they had done so, he said, I am your brother Joseph, the one you sold into Egypt! And now, do not be distressed and do not be angry with yourselves for selling me here, because it was to save lives that God sent me ahead of you. For two years now there has been famine in the land, and for the next five years there will not be ploughing and reaping. **But God sent me ahead of you to preserve for you a remnant on earth and to save your lives by a great deliverance. So then, it was not you who sent me here but God**. *He made me father to Pharaoh, lord of his entire household and ruler of all Egypt.*
Genesis 45:3 - 8 (emphasis ours)

Joseph was able to put his entire 13-year ordeal in proper perspective. Our Sovereign God allowed all the events: the selling as a slave, the lies that were told on him, the casting into prison, and the ingratitude of Pharaoh's servant, as events in Joseph's life to prepare him. It prepared him to be ruler of the most powerful nation on earth at that time, and to provide sustenance for his family back in Canaan and the entire known world.

> **"Only a Sovereign God can weave all the events and experiences of our lives, good and bad, and cause them to work together for our eternal good"**

God inhabits eternity. He sits astride the space-time continuum of past, present and future. He knows your beginning from your end. He knows the trials and sufferings that you are going through right now, and like the patriarchs Job and Joseph, they are all a part of a master plan orchestrated or allowed by a Sovereign God to fulfil His purposes in us.

As another writer, the apostle Paul, wrote:

And we know that ALL THINGS God work together for good to them that love God, to them who are called according to his purpose.
Romans 8:28 (emphasis ours)

Only a Sovereign God can weave all the events and experiences of our lives, good and bad, and cause them to work together for our eternal good.

"Esther" Rehearsals - 1981

King & Queen serenade each other

King presents Queen to Empire

Esther & Jews mourn and fast

Rough diamonds can be shaped by splitting them along cleavage planes. This divides them into smaller pieces to remove flaws and impurities. They are then further shaped by splitting, cutting and grinding

7

PILGRIMAGE IN THE VALLEY

Mike

Shortly after the events of early 1981, we received a package of documents from the United States Embassy, inviting us to apply for permanent resident status. My parents, who had migrated in the early 70s, lived in New York City and had become U.S. citizens. They had filed for all their eleven children. I was the last to seriously consider migrating. However, in view of the personal crises we recently experienced, the package could not have come at a better time. We thought that it was time for a new beginning and to put the void of the past behind us. We successfully attended that interview in May, and in August of that year, the 26th day to be exact, we landed in New York to take up residence there.

The change from the warm, sunny Caribbean to cold, big New York City was traumatic. Pulling up roots from one's comfort zone and venturing into the unknown has its peculiar stress factors. I experienced culture shock. I had always prided myself in my academic achievements, and to an extent that may have seriously been hampering my relationship with God. It was so subtle, however, that I was totally blind to the degree of selfish pride that had become my daily existence and motive for living.

A loving Father knows our innermost thoughts, interests and deceptions. He sometimes orchestrates and at other times He just allows events to overtake us to bring us the necessary mid-course correction that we need to bring us back on track, or rather, in my case, for possibly the first time on the right track. Life in the USA was a learning experience, which was fraught with frustration, disappointment and discouragement.

Our first home was an upstairs apartment of a house shared with my eldest sister Flo, on Bolton Avenue in the Bronx. We were experiencing culture shock due to the vast difference in life styles between the Caribbean and the USA. We found it difficult to adjust to the constant heavy traffic of the highway outside our window, the subway, the fast pace of life, the rebuilding of friends and associates, working styles and the fast food culture.

Getting a job in my field of study, engineering, was as distant as the hills. I remember sitting up one day and night writing applications to companies that had advertised in the newspaper, most of which were job placement agencies seeking to add names to their databank. The prestige associated with being an engineer in a small island was quite different compared to living in a big country such as the USA. For example, being in demand and being afforded the opportunity to pick, choose and refuse job offers was like a rug that was suddenly pulled from under my feet. After months of fruitless search, I had to follow advice and settle for a temporary office clerk job in a bank in downtown Manhattan. It was good to be earning my way, I thought, but what a blow to my ego. This was a big change for me, but through it all we had a tremendous support system in my parents and brothers and sisters. Being a temporary office clerk at a bank is hardly anything I would think of writing home about. I had arrived on my first job with a title of 'figure clerk.' I settled down to do my best, figuring that this stint would be for a minimum duration before something big worked out.

After three weeks on the job, however, Rocky, a slimly built black-haired Italian-American, my boss, asked me to work overtime one Friday evening. This was in October or November. My belief at the time prohibited me from working between sunset Friday and sunset Saturday. I explained to him my reason for not being able to honor his request. He didn't seem perturbed, yet I arrived at work the following

Monday only to find out that another "temp," as they are called, was hired to replace me.

Later that afternoon, Rocky called me to his office and told me not to come back to work. It was so cold, a real slap in the face. It jolted me. In Jamaica, I would have been in Rocky's shoes calling the shots. I felt humiliated in having to return home and break the unfortunate news. That afternoon after disembarking from the subway train, I got down from the 'L' train line and it was raining. It didn't matter that I had to walk a half-mile in the rain to our apartment to break the bad news.

> **"As I reflected on my circumstances, I couldn't understand why God was not looking out for me, especially as I was trying my very best to serve Him"**

As I reflected on my circumstances, I couldn't understand why God was not looking out for me, especially as I was trying my very best to serve Him. I had lost my job to obey His commands, and I couldn't understand what was happening to me. It was one challenge after another. I arrived at my apartment, soaking wet. Everyone could see that something had gone wrong. Or should I say gone right? The Master Potter was beating away at my egotistical pride.

There are some ingrained character flaws like pride and arrogance that have to be corrected over a period of time. It cannot happen overnight. It takes time, patience, trials and testing to eat away at one's overly valued sense of self. I was to remain for several months without a job, as the temporary agency was not interested in placing me anymore. Economic recession was now a real issue in the U.S.A, and the economy had contracted, leaving many out of work.

Sometimes we allow ourselves to have an inflated view of self, and it was some of the people who I thought were somehow of lesser importance that the Lord used to grant us sustenance during these days.

By early 1982 the basement apartment of Flo's house on Corsa Avenue in the north-eastern section of the Bronx became available and we moved to live there. It was a one bedroom studio with Trevor and family living in the 'walk in' apartment and Derrick and family living upstairs. We were on our own. Not being able to find suitable employment, I became so depressed that I hardly had the energy to get myself out of bed most mornings.

On one occasion I decided to fast, to implore the Lord to intervene. That afternoon Trevor, who was a private building contractor, called to say that he had a half day's work for a laborer, if I was interested. I ended the fast immediately and worked for twenty dollars, just enough to buy some much needed groceries.

One day in the coldest, windiest month of the year, March, I left home not sufficiently attired for the weather. I attended an interview in Mount Vernon, north of the Bronx. I had to wait at a bus stop with the wind blowing fiercely in my face. It got so cold that I had to 'mark time' on a sheet of cardboard at the bus stop because my shoes weren't warm enough to protect my feet. I felt trapped. To go back to Jamaica and admit that I had failed was not an option; to stick it out in this wilderness was now becoming a task. The Lord was beginning to turn up the oven and my 'color' was changing bright red.

I had a good interview, and passed the test they had given, but still my non-American experience disqualified me from serious consideration. I began to think of how in my previous employment back home I had sat in judgement of other people's qualifications. Had I refused them jobs on grounds that were probably less than honorable? I mused. I was now in their shoes and learning some very important lessons. Was my past coming back to haunt me, thousands of miles away from home?

From a man's perspective, one of his most cherished possessions is his career, profession or vocation. Take that away from him - his right to earn and feed his family – and you are hitting him at the heart and core of his being. I do believe that the Good Lord built within the male of the species the need to be the major provider for his family, and so there is no more painful emotional experience than for a man to have to depend on others for his existence. Up to this point, I had been living in a kind of self-deception. I saw nothing wrong, no flaw in my character, and so I could not understand why God was allowing me to go so low in my own self-esteem.

At that time, Mike Jr. was just about four and was in need of a playmate. We wanted another son to replace his younger brother Philip and to bring a measure of comfort to him and us. So within a year of our arrival, July 28, 1982, Bev gave birth to our third son, Andrew David. Mike Jr had always wanted another baby brother, so his prayer and wish came through.

The church we were a part of then had taught that women's most important role was being housewives, especially where young children are involved, so there was no serious thought of Bev going out to work.

Our friends Waldo and Judy, who had migrated years before us and resided in Long Island, N.Y., called us. Waldo was financial controller of a small minority contractor specialising in civil works like sewer hook ups, road pavement and drain construction. They were in need of a Project Manager, and Waldo convinced the director that I was the person for the job. Waldo knew that I was in search of employment in my field and thought that this was close enough to engineering to give me a chance at it.

I began working in the summer of 1982. I had to learn fast, because management in a different cultural setting was so different from that of Jamaica. I became acutely aware within the first week that I was like the proverbial square peg in a round hole. I was put to manage men, some of whom believed that because of their experience, class and racial stock that I was unqualified to work over them in a supervisory role. Little did I know that two of them had conspired to arrange my downfall. They resented the fact that Waldo had brought in his friend and given him the job rather than promoting one of them. I had never had to play politics to remain employed, and neither was I prepared to start doing so. One day, five weeks into my employment, these two men, along with some others that they had coerced into compliance with them, botched up a sewer connection, and the customer called the director, cursing and swearing he would drag him into court. My name, which was given to the client by these two conspirators, was called contemptuously to my boss in the argument. I had to personally go to the site and worked beyond dark on Friday evening to restore this man's sewer system, the proverbial ox in the ditch situation.

Waldo called me on the job to come back to the office. There he broke the sad news that I was fired as a result of this debacle. I guess the buck stopped with me. I was beginning to feel like I was going round in circles, spun on the Master Potter's wheel. My pride took another nosedive as I turned in my keys, instruments of my job authority, and headed back home, unemployed.

Through another church brother of mine, Ernie, who was a manager at the fire company in Manhattan, I got a temporary job as a computer aide, an operator of a data communication system for a city-wide fire company. This was the most challenging of all my jobs and proved to be the most financially rewarding one as well. Prior to this, I was joining the unemployment line to receive a weekly check and some hand-outs from the city when the agricultural produce came from the Federal Government.

> **"Without realising it, I had put myself on a religious pedestal and believed that all other Christians outside of my church group were incomplete"**

I breathed a sigh of relief but after a year working there without anything more permanent presenting itself, I decided to quit and return to the Caribbean, not to Jamaica, but to Bev's homeland, Trinidad and Tobago. We thought that this was the solution to our dilemma and so with an air of expectancy, we began to plan to return. We intended to do so in stages. We knew we had to break the news to my mother. One day when she came visiting, we told her. She broke down in tears, for she felt responsible for having enticed us to migrate, only to find failure. I reminded her of her generosity to us, especially during my unemployment months. I reminded her of the time I had hit rock bottom emotionally and financially and she appeared with a bag of groceries and some much needed words of encouragement. I reminded her of how she was like an angel sent from heaven.

Without realising it, I had put myself on a religious pedestal and believed that all other Christians outside of my church group were incomplete for not having "all the truths." So God was beating away at my religious pride and pharisaic attitude.

We completed our trek to Trinidad and Tobago in December 1984. Little known to me, Trinidad and Tobago was in the beginning stages of one of its worst economic downturns in recent years. We looked forward to a new life with new experiences. We tried to put the past behind us, but at times the fact that we had run back to the Caribbean after failing to make it in the USA was tormenting.

Most people would have given up house and land to get an opportunity to live in the USA, where the streets were said to be lined with gold and where opportunity awaits migrants. After all, it is the land of the free and the home of the brave. But very often failure on man's terms is success in God's eyes. God was bringing out the gold from within by denying me the gold from without; that's success by God's measure.

Trinidad and Tobago was a lot more like Jamaica. A lot more similarities existed here than differences. I figured that since my qualifications were earned in the Caribbean, I stood a better chance of finding suitable employment here.

Initially, my family lived with Bev's mother and aunt in Port of Spain, the capital city. I was eager to start working, so I began looking for a teaching job, an area of service that I had come to realise was a genuine call on my life. I had an interview at a technical institute in San Fernando, Trinidad's second city, but it wasn't until later that year that a part-time evening teaching job opened up.

It never rains until it pours, and so it was with our lives. There are periods of unemployment drought, but when it begins to rain, sometimes two or three jobs open up, as it happened in March of that year 1985. Mr Justin Paul, the principal of the institute and the man that I had the interview with, had a colleague who ran a large engineering firm in the south. They were awarded a submarine pipe-laying contract and needed a project engineering manager, and so I was recommended for the job.

I began with high expectations. The project was a multi-million dollar contract. It involved the preparation, pitch coating, concreting, towing, launching and laying of nearly two miles of twelve inch diameter schedule 40 steel pipe, for one of the oil companies. I launched into the project with a renewed zeal. It was my first engineering job in four years.

The remuneration package was good, and we were rented a company apartment in the south, near to the project site. I knew that apart from some minor hitches, the project was on stream, and Mike Mahabir, my director, was pleased with its progress. Despite the layoffs in the oil sector and the economic downturn, this project was bringing in enough revenue to keep my job safe, or so I had convinced myself.

By mid-September we had completed all the coating and the concreting of the pipes to stabilise them on the ocean floor. We had completed all the preliminary stages and were in the midst of launching the welded pipes in stages and laying them on the ocean floor.

The months of September and October were very important to our church. It was the time when we observed the Feast of Tabernacles as recorded in Leviticus 23 and mentioned in John 7. The date was the seventh month of the Hebrew calendar. It was the time the entire church family travelled to designated sites to meet in eight days of convention. It was the most eagerly anticipated event on the church calendar. But at the same time the project work was demanding. It was a crucial time in the project for me, and so difficult to leave.

The launching and laying of the pipeline are the two most technical and potentially dangerous phases. However, my doctrinal beliefs then would not allow me to absent myself from the Feast. My conviction was that I had to take time off from work, despite the crucial stage of this project. I went to the festival.

However, while I was at my religious feast, disaster struck at the work project. A mysterious wind that came from in the Gulf of Pariah one night created giant swells that completely destroyed a length of fifty metres of concrete-coated pipe. The damage caused the endangering of the lives of the pilot and co-pilot of the towing barge. At the time, I was in Tobago, the sister Isle, celebrating the Feast.

On my return from the Feast, on spiritual cloud nine, I was informed of the happenings. I was devastated by the news, and the fact that the buck stopped with me, the project manager, meant serious trouble for me. In order not to distress me unduly, my boss said that as a result of the general economic slide they had to cut staff. I was one of the most recently employed, they explained, and so I had to be the first to go. The destruction of the length of pipe only added to an already critical situation, so I was handed the proverbial pink slip. Once again, I was in the bread line.

> **"I was becoming more aware of a grand design and plan for my life, of which these trials were only a part,"**

By now I was either getting used to this happening or I was growing spiritually or both, but it didn't quite have the same impact as previous losses of employment. I left, however, in full confidence from my employers. I began to be thankful for small blessings, such as eight months of employment. I was not taking things for granted anymore. I was becoming more aware of a grand design and plan for my life, of which these trials were only a part, and I needed to learn the lessons.

The Part-time classes at San Fernando Technical Institute had just begun, and Justin Paul had a few hours per week arranged for me to teach. My parents would always say that when God closes a door, he opens a window. This teaching assignment was our little window that kept us breathing for a while. Justin also suggested that I could again give private tuition. He provided me with my first two students, children of his colleagues.

This venture would prove to be a very worthwhile one, as the classes conducted from our home in Pleasantville grew steadily. At one point, the class was our sole source of income. I had developed a reputation in that part of the country for being a whiz at teaching maths and physics to high school students. My parents have always recited the saying, "God never leaves us without a witness," and Justin Paul was like a witness sent by God to ensure our provision.

But not only did the classes grow, so did our family. On August 20, 1987, our fourth son, William Joseph, was born in The San Fernando General Hospital. We were delighted, for a year before that Bev had suffered a miscarriage. We were living then on Cedar Drive in Pleasantville in a two-bedroom house that had belonged to Bev and her mom. By the next summer, the part-time employment at San Fernando Technical Institute had come to an end. Justin Paul was appointed to the Ministry of Education's head office and later became Permanent Secretary.

During his last year, he had tried feverishly to get me a full-time appointment at the Institute; but the strict nationalistic law of the twin island republic had made it impossible to become appointed, being a non-citizen.

Another door closed, but immediately after, a large window opened. Justin was deputy chairman of a vocational school in Princes Town, and they were in need of a principal and manager. Christ College was a vocational school founded in the mid-sixties by clergymen for the purpose of providing skills training for boys and girls who had fallen through the cracks of the educational system, or were unable to access post primary education. But now the school was in a dilemma. Enrolment had fallen by over fifty per cent, as discipline had plummeted. Once again, Justin asked about my interest in the job. I went to visit the school, and I accepted the challenge.

In July of 1988, I started putting Christ College back on track. I think God was beginning to favour my labors. Shortly, there was a turnaround in the school attendance and discipline, and within the first year, income was realised. I instituted a government-sponsored school feeding program, providing over two thousand meals per week to deserving school children in the community.

Additionally, I initiated a farm project, producing cash crops, and a chicken farm from which we got dozens of eggs daily. The eggs were sold at reduced cost to the community.

At our first open day and graduation in July 1989, Justin Paul, then assistant to the Permanent Secretary at the Ministry of Education, gave the greetings on behalf of the Minister. Mr Paul, in his speech, referred to Christ College as the best-kept secret of Trinidad and Tobago.

God had really begun to bless the work of my hand, for many positive things were beginning to take place. For example, we restarted morning devotion, got the PTA active, and began a Friday afternoon forum where heads of the civic society would come in and answer questions from our students. Within the first year, student enrolment jumped from just over fifty to over one hundred and thirty.

> **"We grow in our spiritual lives with every experience, especially when people treat us with contempt and in return we treat them with esteem, love and forgiveness."**

However, by the summer of 1990, the green-eyed monster of jealously had reared its ugly head. I had done for Christ College what no individual on the Board or otherwise had been able to do. Jealousy, fed by baseless rumours, destroyed my reputation. A few Board members began to say that I had bought a restaurant in Princes Town and was siphoning off funds and goods from the college to my personal account. It was a diabolical lie, and unfortunately the then Chairman of the Board fell for it. According to him, a prominent woman, a church leader in the community, and her protégé, who had worked at the school, seemed to have instigated the whole thing. It would have been easy for anyone to disprove this claim just by checking the facts. However, because of human nature, it was easier to believe the falsehood rather than the truth. The level of stress brought to myself and by extension to my family was high. A government psychologist, Dr Theodore Drew, whom I had counselled with, told me in a fatherly way, "Mike, it's not worth it; for the sake of your family and yourself, resign."

At just about this time, on October 21, 1990, our first daughter Clare Alicia was born in San Fernando. This was one of the happiest moments of our lives! Finally, after four sons, came our first daughter. But even this joy was short-lived, for the outside stress was too much, so I reluctantly resigned. Of course, later that year the truth came out, but I had already moved on with my life. We grow in our spiritual lives with every experience, especially when people treat us with contempt and in return we treat them with esteem, love and forgiveness. We cannot be wrong when we do the right thing, and by forgiving, we give them and ourselves a chance to move on.

On my final day at Christ College, the students came together with some of the teachers and put on a surprise farewell party at the school hall. I was really pleasantly surprised when two of my students dedicated to me the song "*Somewhere Out There*" made popular by Linda Ronstadt and James Ingram.

After an exasperating and frustrating week, it was the kind of send-off I desperately needed. It also reassured me that for the little people who really mattered, I made a marked difference in their lives.

Sometime later, we went back to the USA, this time to Miami, Florida, where my parents and a number of my siblings had moved. During our brief stay there, it was like our lives had come under a curse. Things started heading downhill again, so once again we returned to Trinidad and Tobago in the summer of 1993.

We ended up living in a small apartment in upper Santa Cruz, just five minutes' walk from the home of Bev's mom, who had moved some time earlier to live with her sisters, Carmen and Ena. Our lives had come under the proverbial "up, up, up and down, down, down, then 'round, 'round, 'round." This adequately described our existence. My mother died in October of that year, cutting off any chance of us being able to resume our resident status in the U.S.A., which we had lost years before.

We were now between "a rock and a hard place." Our lives had become an embarrassment to friends and even some of Bev's relatives, who could not understand the spiritual dynamics of what was taking place. I have often said that the least disadvantage of being poor is the lack of money. More devastating than that is the disrespect, disregard and the denigration that is levelled at you in your state of lack.

When you are down financially, suddenly you become an embarrassment to some friends and relatives. You are sometimes ignored and overlooked at functions if and when you are invited, and that is what is so painful about being poor. But it is in hard times you prove your true friends, because true friends stick with you regardless of circumstances. I remember confiding in a friend that I thought that God had abandoned me. I felt so trapped, with no one to help. It is in moments like these that the heat and pressure in the valley bring out the true diamonds in one's character.

Yet again, God never leaves us without a witness, and Bev's mom, Petra, was not only a source of encouragement but provided for us from her own meagre provision. She was like the widow of Zarephath who provided sustenance for the prophet Elijah during a time of famine in Israel. We had lived in an apartment, sleeping on mattresses on the floor and using an old sofa, a borrowed table and some kitchenware.

> **"I learned to identify with street people, vagrants and the homeless, because I believe at the moment of my deepest depths, I was an hair's breadth away from being one of them"**

It is heart-wrenching to see children open the refrigerator door or the kitchen cupboard door and stare into inner space. I remember eating white rice and stewed lentils for dinner once with water to wash it down. Bev's mom, Petra helped in a big way to pay the monthly rent, which included electricity and water.

In addition, we would receive a regular supply of ground provision from "Daddy Jones" of Guyaguayare. Roger, my good friend and brother in Christ, would occasionally offer me a day or two of laboring work. My lofty self-image was still taking a beating, and I ended up doing menial tasks on a job site like shovelling sand and digging trenches.

I learned then to have a great deal of respect for all peoples, even the most menial of workers. I learned to identify with street people, vagrants and the homeless, because I believe at the moment of my deepest depths, I was an hair's breadth away from being one of them. "There go I save for the grace of God," I often say at seeing one of these vagrants. The same blood that was shed for my redemption was shed for them as well. I had no right to disrespect them.

I remember once shovelling sand on a street pavement construction site and thinking to myself, "Why do we humans set up so many barriers — class, racial and professional? In the sight of God, we have all fallen short of His grace and are equally in need of a Saviour, from kings and queens to presidents and prime ministers and to the homeless on the street. Some boastful business tycoons are a pay check away from bankruptcy and poverty.

In desperation I counselled with my pastor, who really had no more insight into my problems than I did. I suggested to him that I felt as though my life was under a curse, which is why nothing ever seemed to work for me. He sneered and dismissed the idea. By then, God had led me to see that we, our church, did not have it all together as we thought, and I was beginning to lose faith in our local church leaders.

So without counsel on the matter, I got an airline ticket from my sister Maxine to return to Jamaica. Two months before leaving Trinidad, November 19, 1994, Stephen Nathaniel was born. Like the children of Israel under Egyptian slavery, the more the affliction, the more they multiplied.

When BWIA Flight 414 touched down at Norman Manley International Airport in Kingston, Jamaica at 11:45 a.m. on Friday, January 6, 1995, I had brought with me all my earthly possessions: a suitcase of tattered clothes, the suit on my back, and four Trinidadian dollars. My friend Dennis had paid my departure tax in Trinidad, and I had left Bev and the children in a three-bedroom Upper Santa Cruz apartment with barely enough food for a week. I came to Jamaica with an expectant heart and a quest for some answers.

The Lord is faithful to His promise. As a loving Father, He disciplines so we do not miss the mark. God resists the proud but gives grace to the humble. Bev and the children joined me later that year, in the summer. Another lesson that came out loud and clear is that the Bible often refers to us as strangers, sojourners and pilgrims as recorded in the book of Hebrews chapter 11 verse 13.

Sometimes God, in His wisdom, allows us to live in extremes, to picture in a spiritual way what we really are in this life; pilgrims and sojourners.

Mike Jr
Playing in snow
Bronx N.Y. - 1982

Camping with Waldo & Judy
Upstate New York - 1982

Mike, Bev, Andrew, Mike Jr.
Corsa Ave., Bronx N.Y. - 1983

Andrew, Bev, Mike, Mike Jr.,
Arrival in Trinidad, Kariwak Village
Tobago - Oct. 1984

Mined Diamonds

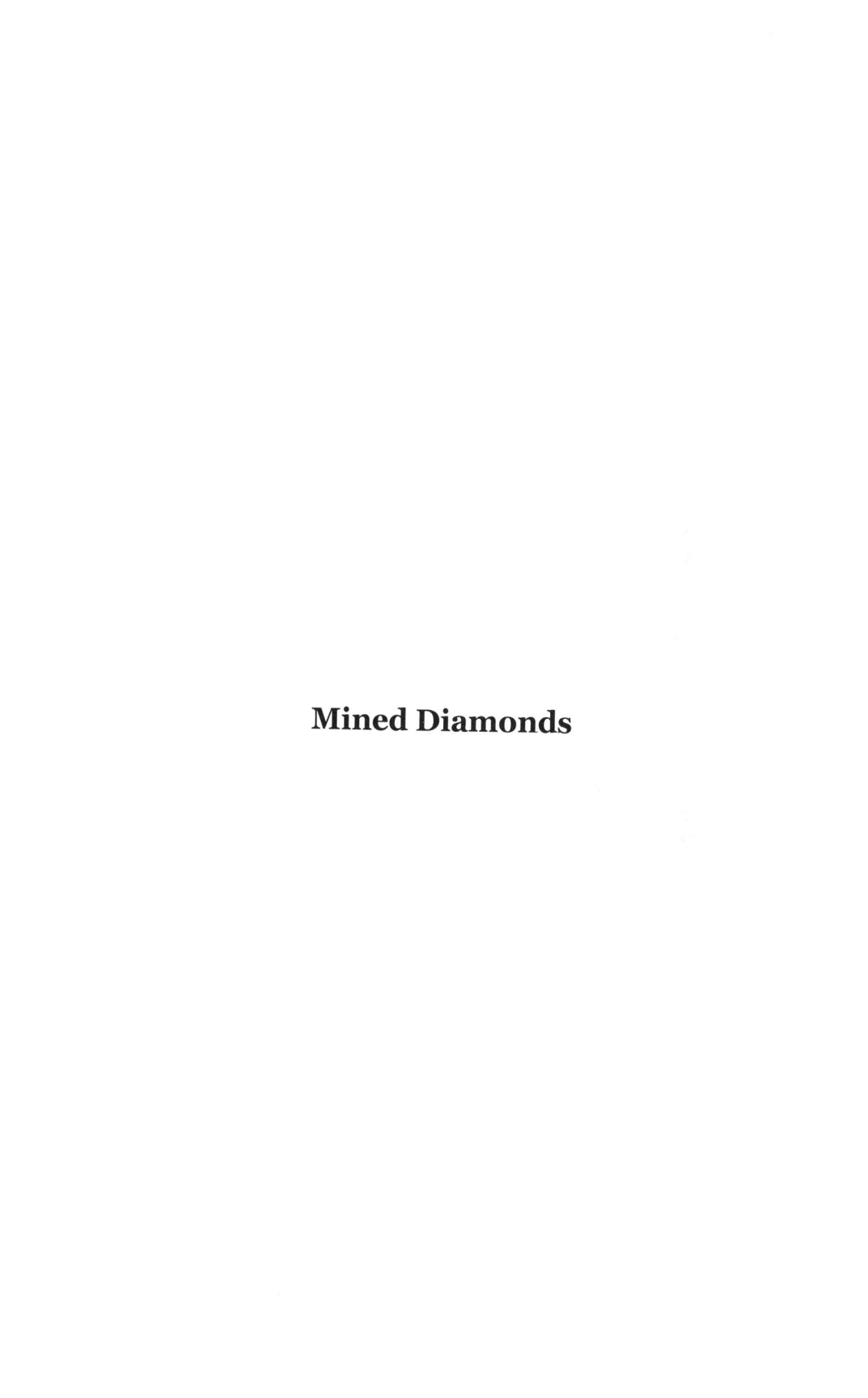

Scientists believe that narrow volcanic pipes running deep down into the earth's interior allow diamonds to be transported to the earth's surface via violent volcanic eruptions.

8

THE CHURCH IN THE VALLEY

Mike and Bev

It would be remiss of us not to mention the significant role played during all our years in the valley, by the church of which we had been members for most of our adult lives.

The genesis of this church, in human terms, began with a charismatic businessman turned religious leader, Herbert W. Armstrong (HWA). In 1934 he founded the Worldwide Church of God (WCG), headquartered since its founding in the United States of America. This Church claimed to be the one and only true church of God, with its roots in the book of Acts. From the WCG perspective, all other denominations and groups fell into various levels of error. The government of the church was an autocratic pyramid with HWA having the final word on all matters of doctrine and policy.

It grew from humble beginnings of nineteen members, and in the early seventies when we became involved in the WCG it had a membership of regular attendees of about seventy thousand on all continents. Thousands of churches and bible study groups sprang up in places as diverse as the United States of America, Canada, the United Kingdom, the Caribbean, Africa, Europe and Asia. Its largest membership was in North America. WCG attracted followers from among Catholics and Protestants.

Among its foundational doctrines were:
- Strict observance of the seventh-day Sabbath: From sunset Friday until sunset Saturday was considered

holy time. Except for genuine emergencies, work was forbidden during this period. The time was spent for religious activities and family reflections.
- Strict observance of the Old Testament dietary laws: The so-called unclean meats of Leviticus 11 such as pork, rabbit meat and shellfish were not eaten.
- Strict observance of the seven Festivals of Leviticus 23: These Old Testament festivals, such as Passover, The Days of Unleavened Bread, Pentecost, Trumpets, Atonement and Feast of Tabernacles were given a new Testament slant and observed.
- Strong emphasis on the deity of Christ: Jesus was proclaimed to be God — eternal in existence, the Word that became flesh, the Saviour of the World and Lord of the universe.
- Strong emphasis on the family: The family was seen as the building block of society. Both nuclear and extended family were seen as the vehicle through which God often works to maintain on earth His witness through the Church.
- A rigid tithing system: This was a system requiring three tithes. The first tithe was used to finance the preaching of the gospel. The second tithe was used to finance the annual Festivals, in particular the Feast of Tabernacles. The third tithe was paid two years in a 7-year cycle, as a welfare fund, for the poor and needy of the church.

Other doctrines and practices included:
- A non-proselytising approach to evangelism.
- Forbidding interracial marriage among members.
- Forbidding marriages between church members and outsiders.
- Forbidding ecumenism among its member churches.
- Non-participation in politics, including voting.
- Non-observance of Christmas and Easter.
- Forbidding the use of makeup for women.
- Non-observance of birthdays.

The church hierarchy was rigid and corporate in structure. HWA was proclaimed to be an Apostle. Immediately under him were several evangelists, many of whom served the headquarters church and taught in the church's tertiary college, Ambassador College (AC), at the headquarters in Pasadena, California. There were no prophets, but worldwide teams of pastors, elders and deacons served the local congregations. .

We could say that a profile of an 'average' 1974 WCG Western congregation could look like this: a mixed congregation racially, ethnically and intellectually; a pastor in his early thirties who may or may not have an assistant or trainee in his mid-twenties. Two elders in their mid to late fifties and five deacons, usually over thirty years old.

"The church policies did not allow for people to walk off the street into services"

The church policies did not allow for people to walk off the street into services; usually, members came in via a subscription to the church's main publication, the Plain Truth (PT). On showing interest in the work of the church, persons may request a personal visit, or attend a PT lecture series, or a personal appearance campaign by one of its leaders. After such a visit and much counselling, they would be invited to regular Sabbath Service attendance, where they would be welcomed to the fellowship of the brethren. Full membership, however, did not occur until a person was water baptized by one of the ministers of the church.

The doctrines and practices had set the stage for insularity and bigotry, and that probably explains why some relatives would often refer to me as being too private and selfish.

The over emphasis on respect for authority at all cost led some of us to be overly controlling towards our children, at the expense of building healthy relationships with them. The bonds of unity and friendship between members and families ran very deep; a true spirit of camaraderie existed. As long as everyone accepted the church's teaching and policies, everything went well. Those who dared to question HWA's authority, or the authority of the local leadership, were spoken to, counselled, or, in extreme instances, removed from the fellowship or excommunicated.

HWA was a charismatic leader who, as a private citizen up to the time of his death, had visited more world leaders in their offices than any other person we can think of. He was a highly respected and much lauded and applauded man who took his interpretation of the gospel of Jesus Christ to more world leaders and nations than any other man since the early apostles.

With all of his faults and flaws, HWA dared to take on the world and be different. He described himself as a voice crying out in the wilderness of today's religious confusion. He dared to be different. One small church of one hundred and fifty thousand members challenged the establishment to discover their version of the plain truth about God.

HWA in his weekly telecast would always encourage listeners and viewers, "Don't believe me, believe what the Bible says." Little did he realize that after his death, on that very premise, using those very words spoken, the living Jesus Christ would come in our midst and challenge us with the same words, "Don't believe HWA, but believe My word."

The church ran pretty smoothly, or so it seemed until sometime after the January 1986 death of HWA. He died at home of heart complications, after leading a full life. He was 93.

HWA's handpicked successor Joseph W. Tkach (JWT) took over as Pastor General and Apostle of the Church. There was an air of uncertainty as this transition came into being. What would the new church leadership be like? Would there be widespread changes? So wondered the membership.

"It was obvious that there were going to be changes in church policies and doctrines - radical changes, a paradigm shift"

JWT was not well known by the worldwide membership. His personality was not anywhere near as commanding as that of HWA. He was more the shy type who preferred the behind the scenes jobs, and was often referred to as the "widows' elder." JWT proved to be a man of sterling character and determination and had been a tremendous assistance to HWA during his lengthy illness leading up to his death. In the opinion of many in the church, JWT was not only just HWA's handpicked successor but handpicked by the Living Jesus Christ, as Joshua was handpicked to lead God's people from the wilderness into Canaan, the Promised Land. However, some church members felt that one of the more prominent evangelists should have been appointed to lead the church; some few believed that HWA's renegade son Garner Ted Armstrong (GTA) should have been recalled to head up the organization.

Within two years of JWT taking over the helm of WCG, it was obvious that there were going to be changes in church policies and doctrines - radical changes, a paradigm shift. Word started filtering down the ranks that all the major doctrines were being put under intense scrutiny by a team of headquarters evangelists and scholars, commissioned by JWT.

No stone was to be left unturned in this quest for the plain truth, and nothing but the plain truth. This move was met with mixed feelings by many worldwide, some with much concern and trepidation. Yet, there were those who welcomed the much-needed review of beliefs, practices and policies. Perhaps one could say grace was challenging tradition and legalism.

"The church, once a haven of peace and unity, was now thrown into turmoil and chaos"

Early 1994 saw the beginning of the paradigm shift. This affected issues such as Sabbath observance and the Feast days, Christmas, Easter, and Birthdays, and it was evident that there was a split right down the middle. Many local pastors did not know what to make of these changes. The church, once a haven of peace and unity, was now thrown into turmoil and chaos. Unsettled and betrayed are hardly adequate words to describe what some felt, having based all their lives on an interpretation of these foundational teachings. Some rejected the notion that the Living Jesus Christ was now smashing every idol and setting Himself up as Lord Supreme of WCG.

Those of us who had begun to see the holes and hypocrisy in the operation of the leadership welcomed the changes. God is no respecter of persons, and what is good for the flock must also be good for the shepherds. Many ministers who had been beneficiaries of the old WCG and the harsh financial demands put on members were now exposed, vulnerable, and began speaking out against the present move of equity.

It was a crushing blow to our confidence to witness some of these men, for whom we had so much respect, turn against each other and against the flock and begin lying, cheating and playing politics just to preserve their own skins.

It was as if the church was turned upside down and the long held and cherished beliefs of the church were no longer valid. We were being stripped naked of our own garments of righteousness, and The Living Jesus Christ was about to re-clothe the church with His righteousness.

During this period, we lived in New York and Miami in the USA, and in Trinidad and Tobago and Jamaica in the Caribbean. So we had been part of congregations of WCG across racial, cultural and ethnic barriers.

In one of these congregations in the early 1990's, ourselves and a number of the members who welcomed the changes were 'side-lined' and 'blacklisted' by an overly autocratic, controlling pastor who was not in full agreement with the new move of the church. Those who aligned themselves with this pastor refused to speak to us, and we were often branded as rebels. It brought into focus what we call the Diotrophes principle in the third epistle of John, where this first century minister was excommunicating the true members of the church and even refused to give the Apostle John audience with the brethren. This pastor seemed to be no different, but those of us who knew that the Living Jesus Christ was behind the new moves, faced the situation with courage and determination.

Both of us, along with a number of our close friends, were gradually removed or were caused to be removed from positions of responsibility. The confusion and chaos that ensued led to many hurts, disappointments and betrayals. Families were split, and even marriages broke up.

Many left in disgust and bewilderment, and the church worldwide was wounded, bleeding and on the threshold of death. Satan, the enemy of mankind, stepped in and instigated some of the very leaders of the congregation to block this move of God in the church. For many of us, this was the most trying of all valleys.

By early 1995, JWT was smitten with fifty spots of cancer on his bones, all over his body. Christian warfare was never one of our doctrinal emphases. Here was a man who in his quest for more of God's Plain Truth, as we describe it, figuratively jumped into a boxing ring naked and without gloves to fight the very enemy of mankind, in defence of this fledgling flock.

The church was powerless against an enemy who sought to divide us, and in September of that year, JWT succumbed to his illness. In spite of all this, he died a peaceful and happy man, and if we could only see more clearly in the realm of the spirit, we would see that He was given a standing ovation by his Lord and Master, Jesus Christ, as his spirit graced the portals of glory.

"The world that we had built around us for over twenty years had come crashing down"

His son Joseph Tkach Jr. was appointed the next Pastor General. By this time WCG was crying, wounded and bleeding from its wounds. Many of its members walked with them no more and have since disappeared from all contact. Some formed splinter groups to return to old teachings. Persons such as our beloved friends Brian and Minerva who were like parents to us during our struggling days in Miami disappeared without a trace from church circles. Others have found healthier churches and have accessed healing and restoration, and have put the past behind and moved ahead with their lives. Can you imagine what that did to our self confidence and stability, to realize that the world that we had built around us for over twenty years had come crashing down?

We walked out of the doors of WCG in December 1995. Then, WCG had less than half its membership left, many of whom were still licking their wounds. There was a dire need for a sweep of God's healing hand. How were the mighty fallen, for WCG once boasted to have had the following:

The widest circulation of religious magazines.
The number one spot in television religious programs.
The largest annual religious conclave on earth (Feast of Tabernacles).
A network of churches that spanned the globe.
A college that won national awards and recognition three consecutive years (Ambassador College).

But in the decade of the nineties, many of WCG's employees were put on the breadline. With the benefits of an Old Testament background and the more recent emphasis on the New, we do believe very strongly that those of us who have been through the WCG experience and who have sought and received the necessary healing and have moved on with our lives do have a tremendous contribution to make to the end-time Body of Christ.

It was sad to see such a disciplined and potentially potent part of the Body of Christ decimated by the enemy. No doubt, he saw the threat to his own kingdom that a Christ-centred WCG could have posed, and so he unleashed all the mustered forces of hell against her. The good Lord and loving Father allowed this to happen to bring about the necessary purging of the church, lest any flesh should glory in His presence.

The lessons from this experience are far too numerous to be adequately covered in less than an entire volume, but central to the downfall of this titanic church denomination were some fundamental humanistic issues, including:

Form without substance is like building on sand.
Purity of heart and intent leads to a healthy spirit.
Never relegate to anyone else ones right to dissent.
Organization must serve the good of the organism.

Organization for the sake of self-preservation is vanity.

He who is the greatest must be servant of all.

Unhealthy spiritual environments lead to spiritual oppression and abuse.

Charisma without character provides fertile ground for Satan.

Today, a vast number of WCG congregations in certain geographical regions that had suffered incredible loss have moved on and are now integrated into mainstream evangelical circles. However, in other regions of WCG, the church no longer exists as a potent gospel proclaiming force, but as a church still in need of much healing from its past. God is merciful and the Lord Jesus Christ still stands at the door, knocking and seeking to enter and dominate, for the glory of God.

> **"Unhealthy churches are insular. They do not collaborate with other churches. Members who leave are condemned"**

In light of this, what should a healthy Christ-centered church look like?

How wonderful it would be, what an example the church could set if all the churches — Methodist, Baptist, Presbyterian, Episcopalian, Evangelical, Charismatic and Seventh Day churches— could all work together for a common good of furthering the work of God on the earth. Very often, however, petty doctrinal and procedural differences keep us separated and suspicious of each other.

Paul's advice to the church in Rome is quite instructive here. In the book of Romans chapter 14 he asks. "Who are we to judge another man's servant? To that man he stands or falls." True Christian maturity therefore includes the ability to appreciate, applaud and encourage the other members of the body who, though diverse in function, are vital to the proper functioning of the Body of Jesus Christ as a whole.

Probably it would be easier to answer this question, what are the characteristics of unhealthy churches?

- Unhealthy churches usually revere one leader who tends not to be accountable to anyone. We should always be alert to the absolute authority of any one person. Be cautious of churches that are so pastor centered, that the pastor's visions are more often spoken of than the great commission of Jesus.
- Unhealthy churches tend to be legalistic. The Bible says the letter kills but the spirit gives life. This must be the guiding light in this area. There is usually a lack of grace and mercy in this regard.
- Unhealthy churches tend to emphasize negative messages. They discourage more than they encourage.
- Unhealthy churches tend to promote cloned people. Such churches do not allow for individuality in members. But there are no two human beings exactly alike; hence each person must be allowed the freedom to develop his or her own uniqueness.
- Unhealthy churches tend to alienate members from their relatives. Be careful when churches put pressure on you to leave relatives and move in to live with their members.
- Unhealthy churches teach that they are the one and only true church. Even the phrase "true church" is a misnomer, as that phrase is nowhere to be found in the scriptures.
- Unhealthy churches tend to invade your privacy. If your privacy is being invaded and you do not have freedom of speech or movement, you are part of an unhealthy group.
- Unhealthy churches quench the Holy Spirit, for they do not equip and empower members to fulfil their calling. The leaders do not encourage members to develop their talents and abilities.
- Unhealthy churches are insular. They do not recognize and applaud other churches for good work. They do not collaborate with other churches.
- Unhealthy churches make leaving a painful experience. Members who leave are condemned.

You may be wondering how any intelligent person could even become a part of an unhealthy church in the first place. But for those who have become members, the facade is appealing. At first the people are friendly. There is a deception that blinds the eyes of the best of us. That's why as long as you are a part of such groups you cannot recognize it. You will need to sever yourself from the group and seek God's guidance before you can begin to recognize what you are in. It is like the idea of being so close to the trees that one cannot see the forest. That is why unhealthy churches have such rigid rules and regulations to keep you from seeing the forest.

It is our hope and prayer that if you have never been a part of an unhealthy church group, you will use these general guidelines to stay clear of such churches. If you recognize that you are now a part of one, seek counsel, for the longer you remain, the more traumatic is likely to be your departure and the longer the healing process whenever you do decide to leave or are forced out.

God created mankind a free spirit. It was never His intention for us to be in spiritual and emotional bondage to anyone or any system.

Feast of Tabernacles - Early 1980's

Runaway Bay

WCG Social - Runaway Bay

Mike Jr & Friend - Mt. Poconos, Pennsylvania

One of the largest diamonds ever mined was about the size of a fist. It was cut into over one hundred stones, representing only a third of its original weight

9

REPATRIATION IN THE VALLEY

Mike

Jason was over an hour late in arrival, and I was getting annoyed and impatient with the frequency of these airport taxi drivers offering their good services. There is one advantage to hitting rock bottom, I thought, the only way from here is up. Humanly speaking, I had been brought literally to nothing: No home, no furniture, no car, no bank account, no money, no profession and no self-confidence. I was even beginning to question whether I would be able to fit in ever again as an engineer.

Life had dealt a heavy blow, and I had more questions than one could find answers. As I stood outside the Norman Manley International Airport awaiting my nephew for a ride to his mother's place, I looked at the see of humanity traveling back and forth and wondered if anyone else would ever suffer the same fate as I had. It is the norm in these developing nations when people migrate they return years later to contribute to their societies. Many educate themselves and their children.

Hardly ever would one return in the kind of desperation that I did. At the same time I began to wonder about Bev and the children and how they were going to manage on their own. My thoughts were interrupted rather abruptly by a shout from the driver's window of a blue 1984 Samara "Uncle Michael!" Jason, my sister Maxine's son was frantically waving trying to get my attention. It was good to see him again. He had grown into a fine young man and no longer the little boy I had left behind in 1981.

I had arranged to spend some time with Maxine in Stony Hill at her place until I was able to work and afford an apartment of my own. This was only the third time I would be back in fourteen years. I came back briefly in September 1988, days after Hurricane Gilbert struck the island, to bring some much needed essential supplies from our church in Trinidad to our sister congregation in Kingston. Then a week later, my entire family came back to attend the annual church convention, The Feast of Tabernacles, which had to be relocated from Montego Bay to Kingston to facilitate the local members. The hurricane, which swept by on September 12 had caused widespread devastation to the island. As we journeyed on the Rockfort road, I was amazed to see the level of development that had taken place. Jamaica had gone through so many changes. There were unrecognizable buzzwords. A new paradigm in music had been established. Even the landscape had changed, and some of the places we drove through I did not recognize. I felt as if I was visiting a foreign land. Would I be able to fit in, I worried?

That Friday evening, Maxine's prayer group hosted a dinner at a Chinese restaurant in Liguanea and I was invited. I got to meet Anne-Marie, Pam, Sonia and some others, some of whom became our close friends and prayer partners as well. They were happy to finally meet the brother for whom they had been travailing in prayer for so long. I got to understand that I had been on their prayer list for many years, especially because of the church group that I had become associated with since 1974. I was eager to get started in settling down, as I had to consider and plan for Bev and the children coming up as soon as it was feasible. The balance of the month of January was spent getting in touch with old college and social friends, and getting reoriented and reacclimatized with the Jamaican society.

There are several lessons I learned during this period about returning to one's homeland after a considerable period of time abroad. There are challenges that have to be met with Godly wisdom and understanding! There is a kind of reverse homesickness similar to the experience I had when we first left Jamaica for New York. I countered this feeling by keeping in touch with Bev and the children by post and occasionally by telephone. The changes that take place in relationships are yet another challenge. Some of the good friends we had left behind when we migrated had moved on with their lives, and there was an absence of the level of closeness we once shared. Relationships are dynamic institutions, and people's feelings and perception of each other change with time and experience. This was a huge challenge to face. There was also a tendency in me to make negative comparisons with our former home. This created unwanted reactions in people who would be expected to be a bit defensive about their own culture. I had to learn to accept the differences in modes of operation from country to country.

The greatest challenge of them all was that some who were my juniors at work and society were now in senior positions. As a matter of fact, an engineer who was my junior by several years in university conducted one of the first job interviews I attended. It calls for a cloak of humility and a willingness to rebuild in all facets of life. Repatriation after a significant time away requires a willingness to start over; as Maxine would put it, "you have to pay your dues."

"I felt a huge burden lift from my shoulders. I was so ecstatic and upbeat I started to walk home"

In early February, I was introduced to Reverend Al Miller at a Christian men's gathering one Sunday at the Medallion Hall Hotel. I explained to him my journeys and my frustrations, I requested a meeting with him and we agreed on the following Tuesday afternoon, February 14. I did not know what to expect, but I was willing to try anything to get this proverbial 'monkey off my back.' He spoke with me concerning my background; he then prayed with me for over half an hour. He literally dared to command every demonic spirit oppressing my life to leave me alone in the name of Jesus. Spirits such as: spirits of failure, poverty, illness and disease and blockading spirits. He also broke off in prayer what he called generational curses, all in the name of Jesus Christ of Nazareth. He ended the meeting by praying for an infilling of the Holy Spirit and said to me in parting that God would provide a job for me within a week. I never heard anyone prayed for me like that with so much confidence and authority.

As I left his office in Regal Plaza, Cross Roads, I felt a huge burden lift from my shoulders. I was so ecstatic and upbeat I started to walk home from Cross Roads to Old Stony Hill Road, over six miles away. Midway along the journey, Maxine spotted me and gave me a lift home. I felt like a new person, revitalized, willing and ready to take on the world. As Al prophesied, I did get a job offer within a week. As a matter of fact, I got a job offer from a former colleague over the phone two days later, without even the need for an interview. I was amazed, as this never happened before. I also got other offers later, one of which I accepted.

I was still attending my old church but started to visit Fellowship Tabernacle, of which Rev. Al Miller is pastor. FelTab, as it's affectionately called is a full gospel charismatic church quite different from my traditional and conservative church group. I began learning about Spiritual Warfare, Christian Authority and Restoration, all in the name of Jesus. These were never taught in my church group; although gradual changes were being made, there was much resistance to these changes at all levels in the organization.'

On Sunday June 18, 1995, five months after I returned to Jamaica, I awoke early that morning; it was the day of Pentecost, and my old church had services that morning at lmmaculate High School. The small choir was performing, and I was leading the group. I got up before daybreak specifically to pray for Clare, who had contracted influenza. Bev had updated me on it in a telephone conversation the night before. I got earnest in prayer, interceding for her healing when, half an hour into my prayer, I started hearing strange sounds coming from my vocal cords. It just came out like a gush of water flowing down a steep hill. It was minutes later that I realized what was happening. Back in February, Pastor Miller had prayed for the infilling of the Holy Spirit.

And it was beginning to manifest in the form of a heavenly prayer language. I was thrilled to put it mildly. I literally fell in love with this new gift, a language I never studied. I would hasten from work every day just to be able to hear myself speak this new language. It sounded like a mixture of German and French. It was a marvel. I called Bev and told her about it. By now, I had arranged for the rest of my family to join me the following month, July.

Things were looking up, and an apartment next to our long-time friends Cleveland and Suzie on Tamarind Avenue opened up so I rented it for $10,000 Jamaican dollars per month. I had to get accustomed to our new currency; for example it took about one thousand Jamaican dollars to fill the green grocer's list for a week. Back in Trinidad or in the USA it would have taken thirty or forty local dollars. As far as jobs were concerned, I had little difficulty finding and keeping one. It was encouraging to be working back in the engineering field. I started out as an equipment and service manager at Gibson Agencies on Haining road in New Kingston in March 1995. I was in charge of the sales and service of several lines of heavy-duty equipment such as Grove cranes, Payhauler trucks and Case tractors. God is a God of humor. I am no known relative of J.I. Case who developed the Case line of equipment back in the USA.

On one of my field trips to Frome sugar factory, Westmoreland, to investigate one of our Case uni-loaders that was malfunctioning, I was accompanied by Duncan Young, a sales representative in the department. On my arrival in the main office, the dispatcher radioed the field engineer on his intercom and stated with a sense of urgency,

> "Duncan Young, the sales representative from Gibson Agencies is here in the office to see you about the Case uni-1oader," he then quickly added "and Mr Case HIMSELF! is here to see you too."

I had a good laugh at that one. I was fortunate and blessed to have had this job so soon after entering the Jamaican job market.

By January 1996 a two-story four-bedroom house on Kingswood road in Stony Hill became available. It was within walking distance from Maxine's place. I still have fond memories of the four years we spent there. This home, nested in the green lush serene upper St. Andrew hills, was the ideal hideaway needed for the sorely needed healing of the inner man.

In July, a downsizing procedure at Gibson Agencies rendered my post and job redundant. At about this time, FelTab was conducting a week of outreach activities in the Mandeville area. One night I was led to share my testimony with the congregation. This was the first time in living memory that I was doing anything like this. I spoke of my years of oppression and of God, my restorer.

> **"Son, one day God is going to use you to take this testimony before university professors and people of higher learning."**

At the end of this talk, Pastor Al's brother, an evangelist, George Miller, met me on the floor in front of the stage. He held up his right index finger, pointed directly between my eyes and said "Son, one day God is going to use you to take this testimony before university professors and people of higher learning." Unknown to me was the fact that on September 2, of that year I would be hired as a lecturer at the University of Technology, Jamaica. Brother George's prophecy would have several fulfillments at different times and levels, as I have shared my life story on many occasions with university personnel.

After years of toil, travel and oppression, God led us to a neat hideaway. On March 12, 1999, our last child Deborah Elizabeth was born. Clare was delighted at last to have a baby sister. Our family was once again settling in and being re-established and reintegrated into Jamaican life. This spacious four-bedroom hillside house surrounded by a half acre of well-fruited land was a fitting "balm in Gilead," to rest our weary souls. Or was it just a brief stopover to rest for the night before the journey continues the next morning? Only the Master Potter knew then. He calls the shots, and we are merely clay in His most capable and loving hands.

Paul's Wedding - Bronx, New York - 1986
L-R Chris, Derrick, Patty, Karlene, Karl, Mama, Paul, Flo, Trevor, Papa

Miami, Florida - 1996
L-R Derrick, Chris, Flo, Trevor, Papa, Maxine, Karlene, Karl, Patty, Mike

Finished Diamonds

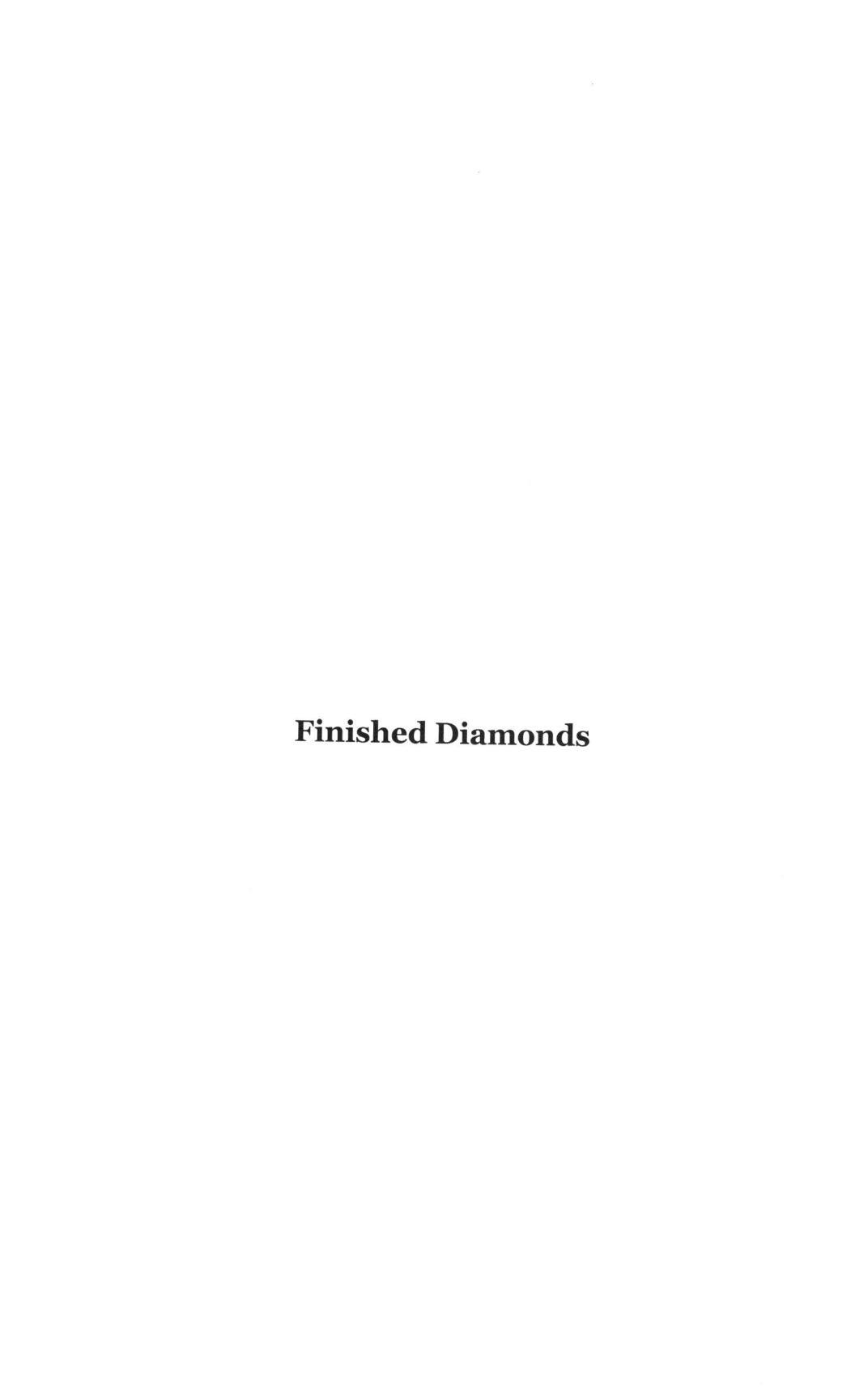

During the finishing process more than 50 per cent of the diamond is lost. If the diamond has many flaws as much as 80 per cent may be lost.

10

BEVERLY IN THE VALLEY

Mike

Bev and I planned that our two daughters, Clare and our new addition, Deborah, and she would go on summer holidays to visit her mom and two aunts in her native land, Trinidad and Tobago. They planned on flying out in early August 1999 and hoped to spend the rest of the month there visiting friends and relatives. Bev later wanted to cut short the visit to be back the first week of September to see William off for his first day of high school.

William had done very well in his Grade Six Achievement Test (GSAT) exams and got to attend the school of his first choice, Ardenne High. From as early as June, Bev had complained of an upset stomach and occasional weakness. The condition was nothing that we had considered alarming, because the feelings did not last. On one occasion, we consulted a nurse practitioner friend of ours, and she suggested an antacid, which proved adequate for immediate relief of the bad feelings. On another occasion Bev got up one night in a cold sweat and with some shortness of breath. It was not in any way a severe attack, and one concern we had was early menopause, which was the case of her mother at the same age; once again, the feeling subsided and there were no further incidents. As planned, Bev and the two girls went on this eagerly awaited trip home, her second home that is. We kept in contact by telephone occasionally. Bev had planned to divide the time equally among her two good friends and her mother. However, things didn't quite work out at her friends, so the entire time, it seemed, would have to be spent by her mom in Upper Santa Cruz, on the island of Trinidad.

On Saturday August 14, 1999, sometime after dark, I received a phone call from Bev, in Trinidad, complaining of an ill feeling. Only this time there was a sound in her voice that spoke to her real condition. It hit me like a ton of bricks when she said, "I want to come home!" It was the sound of one who felt trapped and desperate and somehow the inflection in her voice at the word 'home' sounded so distant and so final. I instructed her to go to the doctor first thing Monday morning and assured her that I would confirm her ticket to return later that week. Her parting words were, "Sweetheart, I love you," to which I responded, "I love you too." Her goodbye was somewhat disturbing; Bev is normally a very cheerful, upbeat person, but that night there was a sombre tone that left me uncomfortable. I mentioned Bev's condition to a number of close prayer partners and tried not to worry about the matter. Other than that, the weekend passed pretty predictably.

At about 4:00 a.m. on Monday morning I was jolted out of my sleep by the telephone ringing downstairs. I hastened to get it before the voice mail took over. Normally, a phone call so early in the morning meant an overseas call; so I didn't care to miss this one. It was Ena, Bev's maternal aunt with whom they were staying. I could detect trouble in Aunt Ena's voice. "Bev was taken to the hospital by an ambulance a short while ago," she reported. She later explained that when she heard the baby crying unceasingly, she went to investigate, only to see Bev on her face in the bed, in an unconscious state. Unable to move her, they had called a close friend, Dennis, who assisted her out of bed and to the ambulance. I hadn't the foggiest clue what this could mean, but throughout the day I thought of our last conversation the Saturday night when she complained that she wanted to come home. It was as if her spirit had sensed something, a tragedy, a separation, and wanted to be back into the 'comfort zone' with her family for whatever would ensue. I could not stay home that day. It would have been worse, so I went to work and on my return, Mike Jr. told me of a message on the voice mail for me. It was Aunt Ena. "Beverly is hospitalized at Mount Hope Hospital with a stroke." I can still hear the trembling in her voice as if it were yesterday. I sent up a silent prayer for Bev and the children and immediately called BWIA to book the next flight out.

The airline flies daily to Trinidad and Tobago, and so the first flight available was Tuesday afternoon, departing Jamaica at 2:00 p.m. and arriving at 8:00 p.m. local time. I alerted my close friends and prayer partners, Carlton, Cleveland, Leaford, Pam, Anne, Marcia and my sister Maxine. I called Pastor Al Miller on his mobile phone; he was stunned, but ensured me of continued prayers and support. I had to take emergency leave from school and get my belongings together for travelling.

On my way out I made a few calls at the airport to others I had not yet contacted. I failed to contact Bev's mother-friend, Lady C. I had earlier updated the boys without too much detail, although I sensed concern in the voices of the older ones. They could manage on their own until "such time." I couldn't help hearing Bev's voice in the last telephone conversation, for her pleading to "come home" had desperation in her voice as she bid farewell.

I arrived at Piarco International Airport, Trinidad and Tobago at about 9:00 p.m. Dennis, one of my long-time best friends was there to meet me. He was very upbeat and positive about Bev's condition, as they had been to see her the same day. We headed straight for the Chaconia suite of the Mount Hope Hospital where we got special permission to visit after visiting hours. Bev recognised me but in her dazed and stupefied condition was unable to muster more than a half-smile.

We remained an hour or so and then I went to spend the night with Dennis and Karen, our long time brother and sister in the Lord. Karen had taken Clare and Deborah to be with them after Bev's hospitalization. It was hard work for her as they had three daughters of their own, ages eight to sixteen. Clare was very much at home with her reunited friends. Meanwhile a miracle took place with Deborah. At five months Deborah had been solely breast-fed. I did not even think about the possible implications, but from as far away as

Miami, two of my sisters, Flo and Karlene were praying that there would be a smooth transition from breastfeeding to bottle feeding. There wasn't even a hitch as Debby took to the bottle like a duck to a pond. This whole incident brought into focus the importance of the Body of Christ as a family. It was comforting to know that in a crisis like this there were people who were willing and able to be all that we needed them to be — brother, sister, father, and mother. From as far as New York, Toronto, Miami, Jamaica and Trinidad, fervent prayers were streaming heavenward on behalf of a beloved family member.

The support and the outpouring of love received by all were overwhelming. Back in Jamaica, the four boys were being supported by other family members. Everyone, especially members of our church's core group like Nigel and Nicole, rallied around them to ensure that their every need was met. Mike Jr. was in the midst of final re-sit exams at The University of Technology and I was fearful that the situation might have seriously affected him. As it turned out he did pretty well under the circumstances, for he was successful in his exams.

"Your wife is a gravely ill woman," the doctor said. "We are trying our best, but we cannot predict what will happen"

Early the following morning, Wednesday, Dennis drove me to the hospital from his home in Petit Valley. I met with Bev's doctor and explained that I needed to know on a daily basis exactly what was happening. He was happy to oblige me. I realised then that Bev had suffered a massive stroke to the left side of her brain, triggered by a heart failure. The heart was only pumping at about twenty per cent of capacity and as a result clots were pumped to the brain, blocking a large portion and rendering almost the entire let side of her brain dead.

"Your wife is a gravely ill woman," the doctor said. "We are trying our best, but we cannot predict what will happen. The next couple of days will give a better indication." I learned afterwards that the fourth and fifth days of a stroke are critical for the patient and often dictate whether or not the patient will survive. I never liked being left in the dark. I've always had the philosophy that ignorance is a curse. I like to be informed even if the information hurts. I am more comfortable dealing with it in stride. So I explored the possibility of over-nighting at the hospital beside her bed, but in the end I was disappointed. To me, feelings of helplessness are severe. At times like these it's hard even to pray because I am in so much turmoil that the Holy Spirit has to minister to me as explained in the book of Romans chapter 8. Yet I was comforted to see old friends visit daily and give their support.

I was still tense when late Wednesday evening Bev had slipped into a deep coma. I felt worse. Her breathing had become irregular and labored. As I looked at her my hopes sank. She was hooked up to tubes, needles and machines on all parts of her body. I could not share with everyone all the information that the doctor had given me. I felt I had to keep a positive outlook. However, the reports were not good. I was fully aware of the fact that Bev's life hung totally in God's caring hands, and that I was powerless to do anything. The doctors had given their all so far. God alone knew all the facts.

On Thursday morning, realizing that Bev was now entering her fourth day, a distinct danger period, I got up in a stupor. I can't remember now everything that took place, but I recall coming down to Simeon Road to catch a maxi-taxi for Port of Spain in order to catch another one to Mount Hope. I had not realised that plying this route were two maxis with two different destinations. One to South Quay where I could easily get another maxi, and another to Charlotte Street a half mile away.

Can you imagine how I felt when I learned that I had taken the wrong maxi taxi? But God is sovereign, and so what seemed to be a mistake, a waste of time and an inconvenience, God would use to fulfill His purpose. Disappointed, I got off at the Charlotte Street corner and walked down Fredrick Street to get to South Quay. All kinds of negative thoughts were bombarding my mind and in desperation I asked the Lord for encouragement and strength to face this. I felt so alone. As I approached the end of

Woodford Square, I saw a Christian record store. From the store there came oh, so sweetly the voices of the Goretti group: in the song *"Sing out my soul to the Lord."* This song ministered to me in so many ways; it reminded me that God understood exactly what I was going through. The fact that I needed to put all my cares in His hand, because he is always with me. And most importantly that His love would see me through to the end.

It had been over seven years since I last heard that song, and it was just what I needed. I turned into the shop, with tears rolling down my face, and I ordered the tape. The Lord would use this anointed song to minister comfort to me for the next few weeks. My mother had often told me that, "Every disappointment is God's appointment." Had I not caught the 'wrong' maxi, I may never have had the level of comfort and assurance I got that morning from that beautiful song.

"It is in the deepest and darkest of valleys that the Lord shines His brightest lights"

God is so good. With a new spirit of encouragement I arrived at the hospital. I could see that the coma was deeper and that the breathing was more labored. Dr Ramphal took me aside and introduced me to the Chief Consultant, Dr Rahaman, a cardiologist. The doctors continually reviewed her condition and updated me. They said to me, "There is nothing more we can do for her. We just have to wait and see." She was now squarely in God's merciful hands. They left the little waiting room and I was once again alone with God. There are times in life when the Lord takes us through dark valleys, but it is in the deepest and darkest of valleys that the Lord shines His brightest lights.

That morning the Lord ministered to me an understanding from John 17 that was mind-boggling. This was the final prayer of Christ, the night before he was crucified. In verse 20, Jesus prays for all believers down through the ages of time. The key verse is 23, the second half:

May they be brought to complete unity to let the world know that you have sent me and have LOVED THEM EVEN AS YOU HAVE LOVED ME.
John 17:23 (emphasis ours)

What the Lord ministered to me in such a profound way was this: God the Father loves me and Bev (and you) WITH THE IDENTICAL LOVE THAT HE HAS FOR HIS SON JESUS. If that truth gets a hold of your spirit, life cannot be the same. As I received it I could sense that the Lord was bringing me into a greater intimacy with Him. I then realized that regardless of what happened from here on I should never question His love and commitment to us. I was again reminded of something my mother often said:

"We need to trust His heart even when we can't trace His steps."

I went back into the ward, placed my hands on Bev and began to pray. After a few minutes I broke out into singing a song made popular by Jamaican singing evangelist Lester Lewis, quoting from the book of Psalms. I innovated by inserting Bev's name.

Bev shall not die but live and declare
The works of the Lord, Amen.
Amen, Amen, Amen, Amen!

As I sang, it did not matter who was watching or listening. This was a matter of life and death. I turned the pages of the Scripture and my eyes fell on Psalm 27.

Teach me your way O Lord, lead me in a straight path because of my oppressors. Do not turn me over to the desire of my foes, for false witnesses rise up against me breathing out violence. I am still confident of this. I will see the goodness of the Lord in the land of the living. Wait for the Lord, be strong and take heart and wait for the Lord.
Psalm 27:11 - 14

I accepted it as a word in due season for Bev and myself. Later that day my sister Karlene called from Miami and directed me to Psalm 9.

O Lord, see how my enemies persecute me. Have mercy and lift me up from the gates of death that I may declare your praises, in the gates of the daughter of Zion and there rejoice in your salvation.
Psalm 9:13 - 14

Bev's good friend in Jamaica, Anthea, sent a card with the following scripture:

Blessed is he who has regard for the weak (poor). The Lord delivers him in times of trouble.
The Lord will protect him and preserve his life.
He will bless him in the land and not surrender him to the desire of his foes.
Psalm 41:1 – 3 (emphasis ours)

As I reflected on all three passages, I could discern that they all conveyed the same sentiments.

Bev's illness was a direct attack of the enemy.

God had high regard for her empathy for the poor.

Bev would live, and not die.

I took courage and faced every moment with renewed faith in all that God does. I have heard that the unconscious person can hear and understand even though they cannot respond.

"I sat by her bedside, leaned over and whispered in her ears. I reminded her of how much little Deborah, Stevie, and Clare needed her"

So I sat by her bedside, leaned over and whispered in her ears. I reminded her of how much little Deborah, Stevie, and Clare needed her. I encouraged her not to give in but to hold on, for we could not go on without her. I learned that afternoon how much of a fighter she is, as she labored to take each breath, with God's help. For those moments she was fighting back the enemy of death.

Later that evening, Dr Ramphal, resident cardiologist showed me negatives of a CT scan they had done the day before. It showed huge areas of dark (dead) cells on the left side of her brain and the swelling and the pressure of the brain against the skull. That was the reason for her comatose state. By this time I was more inclined to believe God's report than the doctor's report.

I arrived at my temporary home in Petit Valley that night exhausted and downcast. I took a refreshing shower, had supper and turned in to bed. It seemed that I had just fallen off to sleep when the telephone rang and I jumped up. By now I had come to dislike the ring of that instrument. I had come to believe 'no news is good news.' Dennis picked it up and said that it was for me. I gingerly came out of my room to answer it, only to hear Mike Jr's voice, calling from Jamaica. The news was bad but could have been worse.

"Dad," he said, "I met in an accident with the car." It later had to be towed away to the mechanic, as it was unable to move. Mike explained that it was raining for several days in Kingston and the roads were very wet and slippery. In Stony Hill where we lived, there had been mudslides. On returning home at about 1 a.m. that morning, from a group study session at a friend's home along the hillside, two dogs ran out in front of the car. Mike swerved to avoid hitting them and picked up a skid that landed him in the side of the hill. He was not injured, but their means of transportation was out for weeks, possibly months. I felt so trapped, so helpless, here in Trinidad and Tobago, a thousand miles away.

The boys, three of them, Mike Jr. 21, Andrew 17, William 12, (Stephen 5, had joined us in Trinidad by then) were marooned on a hillside without any means of transportation, miles away from the nearest bus route. I felt as though I had reached my limit, and I called Dennis and Karen, updated them on the situation and then asked them to pray. I was not even able to pray myself. Both of them prayed in turn what I considered to date was one of the most sincere and wholehearted appeals to God for mercy, grace and strength that I have ever heard. I felt encouraged and left the matter in God's hands. David said, "Why art thou cast down, my soul? Hope in God." I had no more trouble sleeping for the rest of the night.

I can't over emphasize the importance of close fellowship among family members and among members of the Body of Christ as they do their part in assisting each other and being there in time of need, offering words of comfort and encouragement.

The biggest scare of the ordeal, however, came on Friday morning. A young female intern, sombre in personality, requested the evening before that I fill a certain prescription, because the hospital had run out of that drug. I took the prescription, and on Friday morning Dennis drove me to a pharmaceutical wholesale store. The drug on the prescription was half strength of the one available, so I had to call the hospital to find out what to do. When the young doctor came on the line and I explained the situation, she replied in her usual sombre tone: "Mr Case, that will no longer be necessary." I felt my knees weaken, and I was on the way down to meet the floor when she added, "Dr Esack had prescribed something else." I had mixed feelings of joy and anger. I wanted to tell this young lady a few choice words for scaring me that way. I feared calling the hospital early in the morning, for I was never sure of what I might hear.

But thank God, Bev began improving from that morning. Her breathing became more regular, and she opened her eyes a little and even smiled. Yes, she began to look more alive to my pleasant surprise.

Later that afternoon, my eldest sister Flo called from the USA. Flo, a registered nurse of over thirty years was living in Miami. She called, and the operator directed the call to Bev's bedside. It was very reassuring to hear from her. She reassured me of God's sovereign hand in our lives and of the prayers of the entire extended family living abroad. She wanted Bev to be flown to Jackson Memorial Hospital via Air Ambulance, in case the necessity arose.

She had a long conversation with Dr Ramphal at Bev's bedside. He updated Flo on Bev's condition. It was also heartening to hear from one of my brothers, Derrick, that same afternoon, along with Karlene (Beenie), my youngest sister, and Karlene (Cheenie), her twin brother Karl's wife. They were all so concerned and offered their support in whatever way possible.

Bev was discharged from the hospital after spending over two weeks there. She spent time recuperating with some dear Christian friends: Garth, Theresa, Princess and Angela. They were living in Arima. I returned to work in Jamaica, leaving Bev in their capable hands, but eventually, in November, I was able to return to Trinidad for her.

Even in seeming catastrophe, if God's name is lifted up and exalted, then the ordeal is well worth it. On the morning after my arrival in Trinidad for the second time since Bev's illness, we went to see Dr Esack, the neurologist. As we came out of the taxi at the front door of the hospital, a burly, strong, bald-headed 6'6" porter greeted us at the car door. He seemed to be well acquainted with Bev's condition and situation. However, not knowing who I was, he looked at me and said:

"Sir, you don't realize where this woman is coming from. God is good. This woman is coming from death's door. God is a good God."

And as he wheeled her halfway across the hospital to the doctor he proclaimed, *"God is a good God."*

I had always prayed that through it all God's name would be lifted up. Certainly, that morning it brought tears to my eyes to see crowds of people standing, sitting, and working, as Bev was wheeled across the hospital floor, and to hear this loud-mouth six footer proclaim so clearly the goodness of God.

Bev continues to recuperate at home and is now walking and improving in her speech daily. Bev's life today is a testimony of God's goodness, His sovereign nature and His awesome power, and certainly:

Bev shall not die
But live and declare
The Works of the Lord.
Amen and Amen!

....
Since Then

Clare

I'm startled out of sleep by the sounds of carefully contained hysteria. My five-month-old sister cries incessantly, as my sleep deprived, eight-year-old brain wonders why our mother hasn't already attended to her breathy complaints. My grandmother's voice threatens tears as she directs a stranger. In an unsettled trance, I get out of bed to survey the reason for my outsider-induced inability to sleep. Slowly, I wander into my mother's room, unable to look at nothing but the cold, linoleum floor, as my stomach and heart chase each other around my trembling body. After finally working up the courage to raise my abnormally weighted head, time stands still as I see the light of my life lying face down on the bed next to my screaming sister.

"Why won't she do something?" I silently wonder, too afraid to ask. "This is not like her at all."

The lightly veiled terror that has been gradually building within me quickly erupts, as the pieces slowly arrange themselves in my awakening mind. Just as quickly as the realization that something was terribly wrong came to me, the men in white spirited my beloved mother away.

My sister was born on March 12, 1999. Having grown up with four brothers, I was ecstatic that my parents had finally given in to my unremitting demands to provide me with a sister.

"Deborah or Elizabeth," I would say. "I like those names."

And as I spoke it, so it came to be, as my long awaited sister, Deborah Elizabeth Case made her way into my world.
We all lived happily in Jamaica: my parents, my four brothers, Deborah, and I, but my mother was a true blue Trinidadian. She missed her friends, she missed her home, she missed her mother. So in the summer of 1999, my mother, my sister, and I packed up our belongings and flew to Trinidad to visit Grandma. It was just us girls: me and my two favourite people in the world, journeying to the place of my birth. I felt like the luckiest person on the face of the Earth.

As young as I am, I already harbour a strong distaste for hospitals. The only purpose they serve is to remind me that I am just too young. I was too young to see my new-born sister and now too young to see my ailing mother. So I await an eternity in fluorescent-lit waiting room, crammed in with all the other hospital rejects, waiting with bated breath for some news about our loved ones. My sister is still crying. I try to comfort her, while secretly envying her infancy, since her unrelenting cries mirror my deepest fears. But I am eight. I am a big girl. So I push everything aside until I am awash in a comforting numbness. I want my mom, but no matter what, I cannot cry. I have to be strong for my sister, and she has already shed enough tears for the both of us.

My mother was my best friend. She was my hero. There was nothing she could not do. No problem she could not fix, no illness she could not cure, no argument she could not resolve. We were the only women in a house full of men, and as such, we had to stick together. She would hoist me unto her back and carry me around, trudging me up and down the stairs, on days when I was too sick to even stand. She would lift my spirits with her lilting accent and sweet songs and carry me to worlds filled with joy, on nights when I was too despondent to even smile. To me, she was everything.

I don't really understand what's going on. My dad and youngest brother Stephen are in Trinidad now. My dad never smiles anymore. He's here, but he's not with us. The doctors won't look me in the eye.

"Day after day, I retreat to the darkest confines of my mind"

My mother suffered a debilitating stroke. It targeted the left side of her brain, crippling her speech and spatial centers and rendering the entire right side of her body inoperable. She could not move, she could not speak, and the doctors had given up all hope for her survival. As far as they could see, she was desperately banging on Death's door.

I don't like seeing my mom like this; mute, motionless, imprisoned by pristine, white sheets and entangled in the endless tubes of beeping machines. It's enough to break a person, and I do. Day after day, I retreat to the darkest confines of my mind. I escape to a place where things almost make sense. Only in this abyss does my quickly retreating childhood still exist

My mom starts getting better. She is breathing on her own again, and so am I. She is becoming aware of what is going on around her, as she blinks to communicate her thoughts; one blink: no, two blinks: yes. The doctors are amazed. If they did not believe in God before, they do now.

My mom is getting better, and my dad is almost himself again.

My mom spends weeks recovering in the hospital, and Deborah, Stephen, and I are shipped off to live with a "friend of the family" in the interim. He was the stranger my grandmother was directing that fateful morning. I haven't seen my grandmother since then. I'm barely coping with having almost lost my mother; I'm unable to fathom what it must feel like to almost lose an only begotten child, or a spouse of 20 years for that matter. His family is nice. He has three daughters, which under any circumstances would have been a source of joy for me. But since my abandonment, I don't feel much of anything anymore, least of all joy.

When my mom finally gets out of the hospital, we all move in with another friend of the family, one who has the energy, time, and space to take care of all of us. Once we are settled and situated, my dad flies back to Jamaica because although we may be suspended in a time warp, life goes on and bills keep coming.

"I was always an exuberant child; full of endless energy and succulent sass"

My mom is mostly confined to her bedroom, and a woman comes every day to talk to her, to feed her, to take care of her. I avoid my mom as much as possible. Knowing the woman she was, I can't stand to see who she has become. In order to cope with the chaos, I tell myself that this fragile woman is not really my mother. This woman is an imposter, and soon my real mother will come back to get me. Everything will be as it once was. We will all be happy again. But my desperate delusion soon dwindles away, unable to withstand the test of time and the veracity of reality.

I am not the person I used to be. "Madam Speaker" and "Mout'-a-massey" were two of the names bestowed upon me when my family became entirely exasperated by my rolling chatter. I was always an exuberant child; full of endless energy and succulent sass, wholly confident in my mental and physical capabilities. I had to keep up with the capricious antics of my brothers and to secure the parental attention that was rightfully mine. Back then, I was a loud, happy child. But now I find myself suspended somewhere on the uncertain sea between naiveté and knowing, having been pushed through innocence's on-way gate and reluctantly, unsteadily, treading towards maturity's revolving door. I guess the biggest difference between then and now is the silence. The rolling chatter has ceased, and now everyone praises my reserved nature and newly acquired cloak of modesty. I choose not to speak because I have discovered the power of my words. My mother will never be the same again because of me. With my own mouth, I begged her for a sister, and now she can't even use hers. My mom almost died... because of me. Since then, I have carried this guilt around with me. I deserve nothing less. And so, since then, I chose not to speak.

It's September now, and I have been enrolled in the local Roman Catholic School. Apart from compulsory mass and constant Hail Mary-ing, I guess it is okay as schools go. Day after day the vendors stare me down as I scurry through the school gates. They would later berate me for never greeting them in the mornings.

"Yuh muddah di'nt teach yuh manners, chile!"

No. Unfortunately, she never had the opportunity to get around to it.

I am given cab fare to get myself to and from school. My new inhibitions make it painfully difficult for me to successfully hail even one of the elusive, metal beasts. They seem to purposely pass me by, as if I bear some visibly grotesque mark of my sins. As any remaining hope of getting to school on time seeps out of my being, a kind SUV takes pity on me and pulls over. Inside is a girl wearing the same uniform as I am. She looks about my age, my height. Her mother is driving. She talks without ceasing for the entire five minute drive. Her mother is driving. She talks without ceasing... Quietly, I thank them for the ride and hop out, too numb to even acknowledge the vendors' icy stares. I'm late I fall in line behind my classmates and intone our morning prayer.

"Hail Mary, full of grace. The Lord is with thee..."

The next day, and every day after, I walk to school.

Christmas in Stony Hill, Jamaica

William, Stevie, Clare
1997

Mommy, Bev,
Mike Jr., Andrew,
William, Stevie,
Clare
1998

Deborah
1999

Finished diamonds are the most precious of all stones. They have exquisite clarity and clean faceting

11

RESTORATION IN THE VALLEY

Mike

We often feel cheated by circumstances that befall us in life. Having survived over twenty years of oppression, frustration and disappointment, it was high time for a balm, a rest, a time of restoration.

On November 19, 1999, on Stephen's fifth birthday, Bev was flown home to Jamaica. We had gotten clearance from her doctors in Trinidad for the journey and the boys back in Jamaica were eagerly awaiting her arrival. After all, they almost lost her a thousand miles away. Bev, Clare, Stevie, Debby and I were journeying home. While spending time in Trinidad, Clare and Stevie had both spent close to a term in school there. Stevie got some special treatment in flight when the flight attendants learned of his birthday. A special birthday cupcake was presented to him, which he had on board.

This period would call for additional adjustments as Bev was not walking, talking nor attending to her basic needs. With a car that was recently almost written off, I wondered how transportation to and from work and school would be handled. After the accident, Mike Jr. had arranged for the car to be towed to Patrick's mechanic shop on Mountain View Avenue. Initial estimates ran over eighty thousand dollars. The car was fully insured so I expected that I should be mobile within a month or so.

The issue of Bev's care was of concern to me, as I was due back at work, and the children except Deborah were to be back at school. Mike Jr. was now a second year engineering student at The University of Technology. Andrew was a year from graduating from high school at Jamaica College, William had just entered Ardenne High and Clare and Stevie were attending Mona Preparatory School.

Having left WCG we were now settled at Fellowship Tabernacle. After returning the first Sunday we were given a very warm welcome with bells, cymbals, tambourines, and trumpets, with much dancing. After services sister Pam, Pastor's eldest sister approached me and offered the church's services in providing a caregiver for Bev, all at their expense. My thoughts went back to all the years we would faithfully pay 3rd tithe to WCG, now God had begun to restore some of this to us. Some may say that back in WCG we sowed on bad soil so we did not reap a harvest. But God is no man's debtor, as this money was given in purity of heart and mind. God saw the intent, and regardless of what the leaders of WCG had done with it, God saw our hearts and restored what we sowed, bountifully. Doreen remained our household helper for nearly two years, and was indeed a true blessing, one with a heart of service and dedication. Bev's recovery was steady and she gradually regained her speech and much of the use of her right leg for walking, her right hand however is still limp at her side, unable to be used, however it remains normal shape and size and we look forward to full restoration of her arm someday.

One morning in February 2000, I awoke and to my dismay my 1988 white Toyota station wagon was missing from our driveway. I learned that Satan is never happy when restoration is taking place, so he tries to frustrate the restored in the hope that we would give up and surrender to him. It was an extreme test for us to get to work and school and back every day. The missing car was reported but no trace of it could be found. These illegal car-rings steal and strip vehicles in a matter of hours using it for the second hand spare parts underground industry. We were to remain months without a replacement as the Government Agency (FINSAC), which held the mortgage on the car, claimed the insurance check leaving us once again literally flatfooted.

Realizing that it would be a while before being able to afford another vehicle we decided to move from off the hill and closer to UTech and the children's school. It was in April of that year we found a 3-bedroom house in Mona, obliquely opposite Andrew's school and within walking distance from UTech and Mona Prep. Andenne was one bus fare away, so we were strategically placed to survive without a car.

By this time I was elected as President of the Academic staff union, UTASU and was privilege to be a council member sitting at monthly meetings helping to decide the course of the University. I had indicated my interest in the presidency the month before Bev took ill, and even though I tried to back down from the campaign, friends encouraged me to go ahead with it as they would assist in the duties should it become overwhelming. God was giving me the grace to walk through every level of the restoration process.

> **"I was humbled in reflecting on the fact that only a few short years before I had to dig trenches and ditches in a foreign country for a living"**

My mind flashed back to September 1998 when I attended a UICEE congress in Krakow Poland to present a paper on "Retraining and Multi-skilling," that I had co-authored with a colleague. As I stood in front of this audience of the world's leading educators, I was humbled in reflecting on the fact that only a few short years before I had to dig trenches and ditches in a foreign country for a living and now, here I was standing before the world's best, sharing of my discoveries. If God was able to pull that one off, then he could do anything else. I accepted the challenge of President of the union and spent two years in office, having been re-elected in September 2000. God was introducing me to part of His person, Jehovah G'molah — The God who restores. Areas of our lives that were oppressed and restored or are being restored include the areas of Health, Finances, Professional, Social, Academic, Ministry and Spiritual.

I was plagued with several episodes of kidney stones between 1990 and 1994. After prayers were made for my health, I never had a problem with them again. Bev was also on the mend and her heart functions had improved steadily while her motor skills kept steady pace as well.

Our finances were steadily improving. We were able to purchase new furniture and appliances in addition to having a bank account and purchase shares in a credit union. My job also afforded me several benefits like life and health insurance for the entire family.

I had now become an instructor in my profession with the privilege of helping to mould the young minds and leaders of the future. I was restored to my teaching profession as I once taught at this institution in the late seventies when it was a junior college by the name College of Arts Science and Technology, (CAST). CAST had been accredited in some of its flagship programs and was granted University status in September 1995. I had become a member of the Jamaica Institution of Engineers (JIE), A Professional engineer (PE), and a member of the UNESCO International Centre for Engineering Education (UICEE). I had also completed a postgraduate Diploma in Technical Education at UTech in 1998, a Master of Science and PhD. degrees in Industrial Engineering in 2003 and 2007 respectively at FAMU-FSU College of Engineering in Tallahassee Florida.

As President of the Academic Staff Union, I led a negotiation team to the ministry to bargain for salaries and benefits for over 300 faculty members. I also sat at monthly meetings as a university council member helping to guide the affairs of the institution setting and approving policies. I got involved in community affairs and our children's school PTA.

One of the last areas to be restored is the academic area. At one stage during the oppressive years, the thoughts of my mind had confined me to being a trench digger for life with no hope. In my ignorance I had literally accepted this satanic lie. I had missed several glorious opportunities to further myself academically, mainly because of ignorance of God's ways and legalism about the Sabbath days. In early 2000 I had applied for and was awarded one of the most prestigious scholarships anywhere on planet earth under the Fulbright program, and was simultaneously granted two years study leave, one of which was with full pay. This was awarded so that I could pursue graduate studies in Industrial Engineering in a US university. Later on God led me to choose Florida State University (FSU).

On the spiritual front, it was like being led from darkness into light. Our understanding of the gospel of Jesus Christ took a quantum leap and we could now put much of our valley experiences into proper perspective. The Lord promised that if we lose friends and family in the pursuit of His Kingdom He would restore to us many fold. Our friends of the past have still remained friends, however in most instances the relationships have deepened as a result of our new found perspective in God, in addition to which we have made many new friends in different parts of the body. Once the veil was removed from our eyes our relatives and family members received us back with open arms. We do not see ourselves any longer as exclusive Christians but as a part of the ever increasing Family of God.

At this juncture I need to say a word or two about Bev's condition in the overall context of restoration. Bev is slowly but surely recuperating. Her heart functions are all but back to normal; however she still finds walking challenging. She gets around with the aid of a walking stick. What is most encouraging however, are the positive outlook and the peace of mind that characterize her life. Despite her physical limitations, her spirit has gone through a complete renewal during this period.

"God has not given us a formula to determine when and how He will heal in each specific instance"

God introduced Himself in Exodus 15, to the children of Israel at the bitter waters of Mara as Jehovah Ropha, the God who heals. Sometimes he heals instantly and on the spot as in the accounts of the man with the withered hand and the widow of Nain's son. On other occasions, however he chose to heal as a process, over a period of time, as in the account of the blind man at Bethesda, recorded in Mark chapter 8, and Naaman the leper, found in the second book of Kings chapter 5. Still, on other occasions he chose to wait until the resurrection of the dead as in the account of the Apostle Paul and the thorn in his flesh found in the second book of Corinthians chapter 12. The best and greatest of God's servants eventually die, some through natural causes and still others through illnesses, like Elisha the mighty prophet of God in the second book of Kings chapter 13.

God has not given us a formula to determine when and how He will heal in each specific instance. Unfortunately many well-meaning Christians seem to want to dictate to God that He must heal instantly on the spot or on their timetable in all circumstances. They have therefore put themselves under severe psychological and emotional pressures, which of itself often lead to psychosomatic illnesses.

Nowhere in the Bible does God bind Himself to heal us according to our dictates. My prayer is that as children of God we learn to study the bible for ourselves instead of relying on others to give us their interpretation. We may be surprised at how misleading some of the popular teachings of the day really are. God did not design the mortal human body to last forever. Far too many of us are obsessed with the here and now; wealth, health, fame and fortune. In putting our earthly sojourn into its proper perspective we need to come to grips with the reality that one day our hearts will stop beating, and though it will be the end of our time on earth, it will not be the end of us. When we live with our focus on eternity we put premium time, effort and value on spiritual pursuits rather than on material ones. There is no comparison with eternity and our sojourn here on earth.

So if you are not one hundred per cent healthy despite your efforts and prayers, then you can take comfort in the fact that you are in the very loving and caring hands of God and He is in no way intimidated by your illness. Neither is His hand short in His ability to use you in whatever state you are to fulfill His purpose in you. You can glorify God and fulfill His purpose for you regardless of your position or state of life. Do not think you are a second class Christian because of your lack of perfect health. Jehovah G'molah is one of God's names. One that you cannot fully appreciate until the enemy of our souls has stolen all, and God makes restoration. Then we can say Jehovah G'molah, God is my restorer.

Deborah's Dedication
Fellowship Tabernacle - May 1999

The only material that can cut diamond is diamond

12

THE LIGHT IN THE VALLEY

Mike and Bev

David, in one of his most celebrated Psalms, wrote about experiences in the valley.

Even though I walk through the valley of the shadow of death, I will fear no evil, for you are with me; your rod and your staff they comfort me.
Psalm 23:4

In the valley there are shadows because there is light, even the Light of the world. When the Light of God shines in the deep valleys, the shadows may lengthen, but the light illuminates the dark spots and brings hope and encouragement during the journey.

One of the most important truths that guided and sustained us through our treacherous experiences in the valley was the fact that our best friend, Jesus was always there as the Light to guide our path. We did not always follow that light, but whenever we did, we benefitted. Who is this Light, Jesus? To respond meaningfully, we must go back at least two thousand years, for He came into this world in the autumn of about 5 BC. He was born in Bethlehem of Judea. He lived a spotless, sinless life, having been miraculously conceived by the Holy Spirit and born of a virgin's womb. Jesus Christ of Nazareth, Messiah, Emmanuel, God in the flesh, Lord and Saviour of all mankind walked this earth for over thirty three years.

The pages of history; sacred and secular, bear record of His deeds of healing the sick, raising the dead and preaching the gospel to the poor.

On Nisan 14 (April 6) AD 30, just after sunset in accordance with Jewish tradition, Jesus and His disciples sat down to supper, the Passover meal, in the Upper Room. The time had come for the fulfillment of the words of the prophets of old that foretold of the Suffering Servant of God who would pay the penalty incurred by your sins and mine.

After the traditional Passover meal, Jesus instituted the New Testament Passover, Communion Meal, or Lord's Supper, with unleavened bread and wine. At about midnight Jesus was arrested by a band of soldiers, prompted by the betrayal of Judas, one of His disciples. He was dragged before the Sanhedrin, the Jewish Council of the day, and tried, then subsequently sentenced in a 'kangaroo court.' Jesus was found guilty of blasphemy and sentenced at night, delivered to the guards who spat on Him, insulted Him, slapped Him in the face and otherwise abused Him.

And the men that held Jesus mocked him, and smote him. And when they had blindfolded him, they struck him on the face, and asked him, saying, Prophesy, who is it that smote thee? And many other things blasphemously spake they against him.
Luke 22:63 - 65 (KJV)

Jesus had no sleep that night and nothing to eat. No one knows or probably will ever know the extent to which He suffered and for how long, but early next morning, April 7, he was delivered to Pilate, where he was tried, and although found innocent, was flogged and delivered into the hands of a mob to be put to death by crucifixion.

Then Pilate took Jesus and SCOURGED him and the soldiers platted a CROWN OF THORNS and put it on his head, and they put on him a purple robe, and said, Hail, King of the Jews! And they smote him with their hands.
John 19:1 - 3 (KJV, emphasis ours)

A Roman scourge was a whip made of heavy animal hide. Awful treatment was meted out to the crucified with the intent of causing them shame. Victims of crucifixion were first flogged until weak and bleeding profusely. The whip had nine tails, each of which had attached at the end pieces of bone or metal. The result of each lash was that a piece of flesh was plucked from the back, leaving the impression of a furrowed field.

In addition, a crown of thorns was platted and imposed on His head. These thorns could have varied in length between two and four inches. This evidently caused excruciating pain as the thorns penetrated His scalp. After a series of trials, Jesus was handed over to a mob to be crucified at about 9 am. Jesus was then so weak from His nightlong ordeal, with His body beaten, battered and bloodied that Simon, a Cyrenian, was commanded to bear His cross to the place of crucifixion, called Golgotha or Calvary as recorded in the book of Mark chapter 15.

"Crucifixion was the most shameful form of capital punishment reserved for slaves and the worst of criminals"

Crucifixion is not a modern day means of capital punishment, so we need to go back in the pages of history to get a clearer picture of what took place that day.

This form of capital punishment was invented by the Phoenicians for the purpose of severely punishing criminals. This was accomplished by a slow and painful death on the cross as well as their state of nudity. The Romans later adopted this form of capital punishment to deter crime in the empire. They made several modifications to it, including driving spikes through the hands and feet of the crucified. This ensured that the process would not take days but hours.

Crucifixion was the most shameful form of capital punishment reserved for slaves and the worst of criminals. Survival on the cross depended largely on the legs, the portion between the ankle and the knee. This part of the human anatomy is used as a column support to push the victim up in order to breathe, otherwise suffocation takes place. That is why as the Sabbath drew nigh at sunset and the

Jews did not want the victims to remain on the cross after sunset, they requested of Pilate that the legs of the prisoners be broken, so that not being able to push up and breathe, they would die in a matter of minutes.

However, to fulfil all prophesies that not a bone was broken of the Passover Lamb as detailed in Exodus chapter 12, Jesus was already dead when they came. To be absolutely sure that He was really dead, the attending soldier ran a spear through His side, from where came blood and a clear liquid.

One prophetic passage of scripture, Psalm chapter 22, details with fine accuracy the suffering of Jesus the Messiah. With amazing accuracy a Roman form of capital punishment was detailed by a Jewish prophet hundreds of years before the event. Psalm chapter 22 verses 1 to 10 gives the setting as the crucifixion of Christ:

I am poured out like water.
Verse 14 (first phrase)

In the midday sun Jesus perspired so profusely that verse 15 says His strength was dried up, and His tongue stuck to the roof of His mouth. On one occasion He said, "I thirst," since the human body is over seventy per cent water, when one becomes dehydrated one's strength is dried up.

My heart has turned to wax; it has melted away
within me.
Verse 14 (third phrase)

As a result of the lack of oxygen, due to the difficulty in breathing, His heart would go into involuntary spasms and even suffer cardiac arrest. For portions of time there would also be erratic palpitations and from His point of view it appeared as if His heart was falling apart. His suffering was extreme, more than any man had ever suffered. Most significant on that day was the period between noon to 3 pm. Luke, the first century historian and disciple of Jesus, wrote in his biography of the Messiah:

It was now about the sixth hour, and darkness
came over the whole land until the ninth hour,
for the sun had stopped shining.
Luke 23:44 - 45

Secular history also bears witness to this event. Phlegon a Greek writer who lived in the second century AD wrote that there was a great darkness over Europe, surpassing anything that had ever been seen. At the same time an earthquake had caused much damage in the area. Tertullian a prolific writer of the second and third century also said later that he found in the records of Rome evidence of unexplained worldwide darkness.

As light is symbolic of Divine Presence, darkness is similarly symbolic of God removing His presence. This period in the process of redemption is very important. The Apostle Paul wrote;

God made him who had no sin to be sin for us so that in him we might become the righteousness of God.
2 Corinthians 5:21

As Jesus hung on the cross battered and bleeding a divine edict was issued, a divine order was made that all the sins of mankind - past, present and future - should be embodied in that suffering mass of flesh and bone.

No other human being has ever felt the full wrath of God. We need to understand something about the nature of God. He is total Love, but also totally uncompromising regarding sin. A Holy God cannot push sin under the proverbial carpet as we humans often do. So all the judgments and all the wrath of a Holy God fell on sin that day.

"As sin hung suspended between heaven and earth God turned His back and removed His presence"

As sin hung suspended between heaven and earth God turned His back and removed His presence. At this point in time, Jesus, now the sin bearer, hung alone. You and I have never been alone. God's ironclad promise to us ensures against aloneness.

However, Jesus never had that promise, for God knew that when Christ became sin, that eternal fellowship they both enjoyed would have to be broken, and Christ made to suffer by Himself totally as written in the book of Hebrews chapter 1. Jesus hung suspended between heaven and earth, totally alone. The night before, one disciple had betrayed Him, another had denied Him, and the others had forsaken Him and fled. Apart from John the beloved, and some of the women who were at a distance, He hung alone. The Holy Spirit was not yet given and the holy angels did not minister to Him. The only other active beings around the cross that day were recorded in Psalm, the 22nd chapter.

Do not be far from me, for trouble is near and there is NO ONE to help. Many bulls surround me, strong bulls of Bashan encircle me. Roaring lions tearing their prey open their mouths wide against me.
Psalm 22:11 - 13 (emphasis ours)

The demonic hordes of hell were on the scene that day. Not just any demon, but 'Strong Bulls,' the top flight lieutenants in the army of darkness. They encircled the cross like vultures going in for the kill.

Open their mouths wide against me.
Verse 13 (second phrase)

This is better translated gape or taunt. These demons and evil spirits taunted the suffering Jesus Christ. In our opinion their taunts might have been like this;

"Give up Jesus, it's not worth it, forget about this salvation thing, throw in the towel, you're crazy. You called him your father and at the most critical time of your life he has deserted you, curse him and die."

Dogs surround me, a pack of villains encircled me; they pierce my hands and my feet.
Verse 16

Gentile Roman soldiers fulfilled this part of the prophecy.

All my bones are on display.
Verse 17 (first phrase)

Could it be that the all-night abuse and the scourging the following morning left His flesh so torn from His body that His rib cage was exposed to the elements?

Another one of the prophetic passages on the suffering Messiah, The book of Isaiah chapters 52 and 53 reads:

His appearance was so disfigured BEYOND that of any man, and his form marred BEYOND HUMAN LIKENESS.
Isaiah 52:14 (emphasis ours)

"There was never a man as disfigured as Jesus was, and at His death He did not anymore bear the resemblance of a human being"

What this passage is clearly showing is that when all was said and done and Jesus bowed His head and gave up the spirit that afternoon, of all the atrocities of World Wars I & II, Korea, Vietnam, Desert Storm, Afghanistan and Iraq, there was never a man as disfigured as Jesus was, and at His death He did not anymore bear the resemblance of a human being. Jesus hung battered and bleeding with His flesh torn from His body, deserted and forsaken by all, with the hordes of hell inflicting heavy spiritual and emotional blows on Him. He had never, humanly speaking, perceived the day when the Father would turn His back on Him.

The evening was still and dark. A quiet gentle wind blew over His now fly infested body. It was as if time had stood still. For a moment the space-time continuum seemed to have been interrupted as heaven, hell and earth waited with bated breath. This was the most momentous event in the entire history of the universe.

Jesus' head hung with His chin touching His chest. By now His strength was fast waning. The mental and emotional agony would have been too much for the strongest of us. There was no one there to offer a word of encouragement, so He had to encourage Himself.

His lips started moving as He began speaking out His thoughts, and in His dying moments, as His Spirit began to take its leave of His body, He looked down through the corridors of time into our twentieth century. In a little village in Kingston, Jamaica He witnessed the birth of a baby boy on the 7th day of the 7th month, and as this new life cried its way into its earthly sojourn, Jesus looked on him with much love and compassion and said to Himself:

Someday that boy is going to need a Saviour. Some day he will need a friend to walk side by side with him through the dark and lonely valleys. I cannot let him down. I have to be there for him. I have to be there for baby Mike.

With a renewal of spirit and energy, Jesus raised His head, looked heavenward and shouted *"TETELESTAI!"* meaning "It is Finished!" or just "Finished!" He then added: *"Father, into your hands I commend my spirit."*

As space and time continued;
Heaven sighed a sigh of relief.
Earth finally had a Redeemer.
All hell was thrown into chaos.

Jesus Christ of Nazareth
Pure and Spotless Lamb of God
Conquering Lion of the tribe of Judah
Son of God, Son of man, Son of David
Almighty Creator of the Universe
!!The Alpha and the Omega!!
The Beginning and the End
Wonderful Counsellor
!!!The Mighty God!!!
Everlasting Father
!Prince of Peace!
Good Shepherd
Emmanuel
Messiah
Friend
of Mike and Bev

At 3:00 pm on the 14th day of Nisan (April 7) AD 30, on behalf of the entire human race and in our stead, Jesus died the death of a common criminal in Palestine, humanly speaking. He died carrying with Him all the burdens, sins, sicknesses and diseases of all humanity, and in the process triumphing over the powers of darkness.

The pages of history bear record that Jesus Christ of Nazareth walked out of the tomb on the third day and today He lives forevermore in Heaven's resplendent glory to make intercession on our behalf.

Because Jesus died, and lives, there is light in the valley, light in the deepest and darkest parts. His death and resurrection makes possible for us experiences in the valley that are like most brilliant and precious of diamonds to shine forever in radiant glory.

> **"Jesus has paved the way for all mankind to shake off the grave clothes of despair, discouragement and defeat and walk triumphantly in and through life's valleys"**

Jesus has paved the way for all mankind to shake off the grave clothes of despair, discouragement and defeat and walk triumphantly in and through life's valleys.

Some time ago as we were meditating on two passages of scripture detailing the sufferings of Jesus and trying to reconcile the roles of Christ; on the one hand as Suffering Servant and Sin Bearer and on the other hand as High Priest and Advocate. The Lord ministered to us something in the form of a poem we now share:

If you were born in poverty, a ghetto or simply in a horses' stable, take it to Jesus, He's been there.

If you have been hungry and naked with nowhere to lay your head, take it to Jesus, He's been there.

If you have suffered persecution and discrimination on the job, take it to Jesus, He's been there.

If you have been misunderstood, misrepresented and mistreated, take it to Jesus, He's been there.

If your friends deserted you when you needed them the most, take it to Jesus, He's been there.

If you were rejected, despised, insulted and spat upon unjustly, take it to Jesus, He's been there.

If you have been lied about, misjudged and delivered to evil men, take it to Jesus, He's been there.

If your spouse mistreated you, abused you and nailed you to a tree, take it to Jesus, He's been there.

If your father abandoned you at the most critical period in your life, take it to Jesus, He's been there.
Whatever valley you have been through, take it to Jesus, He's been there.

Jesus our friend paid the ultimate penalty for the redemption of all mankind. What are you doing about that? With Him you will have light in the valley of life, for as it is written; He is the Light; the Way, the Truth and the Life.

EPILOGUE

The dynamics of suffering, trials and testing are too important to the Christian experience to be overlooked. It is far easier to sweep such discussions under the proverbial carpet and assume that all is well and rosy. For those of us for whom suffering is a present reality, then there is hope, for the word of God is replete with testimonials from the experiences of the saints.

Visit our website at *diamondsinthevalley.wordpress.com* for open discussion on our blog, and feel free to share your thoughts and your life's journey with us.

Made in the USA
Lexington, KY
15 November 2013